D1879727

PRISONS AND SOCIETY

A Study of the Indian Jail System

Prisons and Society

A Study of the Indian Jail System

By

Jaytilak Guha Roy

GYAN

Prisons and Society
A Study of the Indian Jail System

© Jaytilak Guha Roy

ISBN : 978-81-212-0243-5

All rights reserved. No part of this book may be reproduced in any manner without written permission

First Published 1989, Reprint 2013 in India by
Gyan Publishing House
23, Main Ansari Road, Daryaganj,
New Delhi - 110002
Phones : 23282060, 23261060

Fax : (011) 23285914
E-mail: books@gyanbooks.com
website: gyanbooks.com

Printed at : Sagar Color Scan, New Delhi.

DEDICATED

To

The Sacred Memory of

My Father

NAGENDRA KUMAR GUHA ROY

Who

Suffered Imprisonment

For A Decade

For

INDIA'S FREEDOM

FOREWORD

"The mood and temper of the public with regard to the treatment of crime and criminals is one of the most unfailing tests of the civilisation of any country"

Winston Churchill

Restriction on movement by confining the individual in defined precincts as a mode of punishment became common during colonial days. Macaulay's Penal Code, save for death penalty in some specified offences, largely prescribed various terms of imprisonment for different offences, prescription being of maximum sentence that Court can impose, leaving to the discretion of Presiding Officer to determine the quantum of sentence proportionate to the gravity of the offence charged. In ancient times, punishment by imprisonment was very uncommon as is evident from the fact that ancient Codes rarely mentioned it (p. 5). In ancient times, and right up to the Moghul period, punishment took the form of torture and the underlying philosophy was "a tooth for a tooth and an eye for an eye". Modern approach towards this type of punishment inflicting human torture as barbaric and wholly unrelated to the object underlying punishing a criminal. Even now, capital punishment smacks of the remnant of the by-gone days because it is nothing short of limb for limb approach. There is strong movement for its abolition, on the ground that it is a cruel and unusual punishment as prohibited by the American Constitution. And yet, there are countries which justify such barbaric punishment as stoning to death one guilty of adultery.

The goals of punishment have been undergoing radical changes contemporaneous with the wider awakening about the rights of even wrong doers. Crime is the outcome of a diseased mind and jail must have an environment of hospital for treatment and care of mental disease. This approach eschews the deterrent and retributive elements of punishment and strongly advocates reformative approach.

The leaders of the movement of independence of our motherland repeatedly suffered incarceration at the hands of imperial rulers. And prison under foreign rulers was "The Gaol a place of dread". One can recall the horror of detention in Visapur jail of political prisoners of 1932 movement. The barbaric treatment, dehumanizing atmosphere, human torture and wholly unhygienic food made Visapur a place of dread. It was, therefore, legitimately assumed that the leaders of movement of independence who became rulers of independent India would accord highest priority to prison reforms by converting them from institution of horror to modern reclamation and correctional centres.

And yet, four decades after independence, we are governed by the antediluvian Prison Act of 1894. Imperial days jail Manuals have hardly undergone any noteworthy change even after a Model Prison Manual was drawn up, largely relying upon the recommendations of the First Congress in the Prevention of Crime and Treatment of Offenders. But nothing concrete emerged justifying a cynical belief that committees are appointed to avoid doing anything about the problem handed over to committee. The latest is the unattended voluminous report of Mulla Committee. The number of committees set up by the Central Government and the various States is legion. They have produced voluminous report. And, as usual, they are gathering dust in some pigeon holes. And prison continues to be the place of dread.

As late as 1979, when the notorious criminal Charles Shovebhraj drew the attention of the highest court in the land to the appalling and gruesome condition prevailing in Tihar jail in the capital compelling three Justices of the Supreme Court to visit that Institution that the iron curtain separating the citizen from some of their colleagues, was pierced revealing the ugly dehumanised institution, called jail. This ugly situation was exposed as late as 1978. The life in jail was described as animal existence which was an understatement in asmuch as cattle roam about without fetters while some prisoners are kept in fetters twenty four hours a day and thirty days a month, at the discretion of the Superintendent. Is this a reformative approach ?

Art. 21 of the Constitution forbids deprivation of personal liberty except according to the procedure prescribed by law. This law has to be fair, just and reasonable. Can anyone say that the executive fiat called Jail Manual and Prison Act of 1894 prescribe law as just, fair and reasonable ? The statute of 1894 vintage would reflect the mores of the day where words just fair and reasonable were not on the horizon.

The author has vividly drawn attention to the myriad problems that call for attention for prison reforms. Open air prison is being experimented with. But what is forgotten is that sentence attaches a stigma to the criminal and even after he suffers sentence and repays debt to the society, the stigma remains ineffaceable. The approach requires reevaluation.

Further classification of prisoners based on the so-called social status strikes at the root of equality principle. A poor person who may commit crime out of compelling necessity still suffers inequality before law. A richman who thrives at the cost of society enjoys privilege in jail by being classified 'A' prisoner. This classification may not stand the test of Art. 14. The outdated mode of classification deserves to be scrapped.

Political prisoners and conscientious objector must get a differential treatment. Basic changes are called for in this behalf.

The author has presented the problem for energizing the conscience of the society towards the neglected segment of our society.

D.A. Desai
Former Judge. Supreme Court of India
Former Chairman Law Commission of India

Surat
February 1, 1989

PREFACE

For a long time until the beginning of the present century criminals were looked with hatred, and society's reaction to crime was entirely retributive and punitive. The humanitarian social reformers of the civilized world have of late and very rightly been showing great concern for the reformative treatment of offenders. The progressive governments, particularly in the West, are now experimenting and implementing various schemes for prison reforms on grounds of social utility as well as humanitarianism. It is extremely unfortunate that in India, even four decades after freedom, the ghost of the British Raj still haunts our prisons more than any other institution. Much needed jail reforms are still pending despite the zeal of our great national leaders who spent long years in prisons during the trying days of India's struggle for freedom and thus experienced the horrors of prison life. No wonder prisons in India continue to serve as breeding places for hardened criminals rather than the correctional institutions as they should be. Official apathy and paucity of funds are indeed the great stumbling blocks to effective jail reforms. But, there are many other constraints which must be courageously faced if we really want our jails to become reformation centres. It is this feeling which inspired me to choose jail administration as the subject of my doctoral dissertation. The present book is based on this dissertation which has been approved by the University of Calcutta.

The central figure in jail administration in every country is the most complicated product of our modern civilization—the criminal. The problems of jail administration throw up many more psychological, sociological, ethical, legal, political and economic issues than those of any other branch of public administration. This book is a modest endeavour to grapple with these problems in relation to operation of prisons in the Indian society and to suggest suitable ways and means for their solution.

I take this opportunity to record my profound sense of gratitude to my respected teacher late Dr. Ramesh Chandra Ghosh, former Centenary Professor of Public Administration in the University of Calcutta, for his unstinted encouragement and guidance in conducting this study. I recall with delight the illuminating discussions I was fortunate to have with him at every stage of my work. It remains for me a personal tragedy that I failed in presenting a copy of this book to him.

For getting myself acquainted with the practical side of prison administration, I visited a number of jails in West Bengal. Special thanks are due to the State Government which was kind enough to provide me with all facilities for that purpose.

I should also record my indebtedness to Shri Sukhamoy Dutt, Chairman of the West Bengal Jail Code Revision Committee of 1972-73, Smt. Sudha Mazumdar, a distinguished social worker, and several authorities and agencies, both at home and abroad, notably the American Correctional Association, the National Institute of Social Defence, the National Library, the West Bengal Secretariat Library for rendering indispensable assistance in many ways for the completion of my work.

I owe a special debt of gratitude to Hon'ble Justice D.A. Desai, former Chairman, Law Commission of India who has been kind enough to write a foreword for this book. His foreword must have added a few illuminating pages to the book.

I am indebted to my wife, Shibani, for giving me continuous encouragement. My little son, Rajtilak, stood patiently the deprivation of his father's company most of the time for which his indirect contribution to the work needs special acknowledgement. Thanks are due to Smt. Latika Panesar for preparing the type-script. I also owe a special debt of gratitude to Shri B.P. Garg and Shri A.P.S. Chauhan of the Gian Publishing House who have been responsible for converting an idle man into an active one.

Indian Institute of Public Administration
New Delhi—110002

JAYTILAK GUHA ROY

CONTENTS

1

PRISON ADMINISTRATION IN INDIA : HISTORICAL RESUME

The prison administration of a country is a function of several variables pertaining to socio-economic conditions and practical considerations. The socio-economic conditions vary from one country to another and have immense influence on the plans, programmes and policies of a country's prison administration. The funds available to a developing country for meeting the requirements of its prison administration could never be more than that of a developed country so that the pattern of social defence would inevitably differ from each other. Again, an increase of a country's national income may often be followed by an additional expenditure on its prisons. But whether or not such increased expenditure would reduce the number of crimes or the size of prison population must necessarily depend upon the nature of resource-allocation in the jail-budget in addition to various economic, social and political factors. Thus, for a society like ours where economic disparities are widespread, distribution of wealth is inequitable, problem of unemployment is acute and the urge for development of the individual self is almost subdued, it would not be unnatural if for some years crime-figures in our country tend to rise despite efforts, whatever there be, at prison-reforms.

The purposes of a country's prison administration are, therefore, determined, apart from its financial capability, by social and moral consciousness of the community concerned. For a long time until the close of the nineteenth century criminals were looked with hatred, and social reaction to crime was entirely retributive and punitive. The purpose of prison administration was then to reform the criminal, if at all, "through the discipline of punishment". But, with the passage of time as well as the progress of human civilization, the humanitarian considerations became increasingly dominant in the matter of society's dealing with criminals. And today, these considerations have reached such a height that crime is considered a social disease and the criminal its victim. The *punitive* reaction is thus replaced by a new *scientific*, societal approach in which "the criminal is treated rather than punished".[1] The following is a reflection of this new approach :

> Imprisonment and punishment do not present themselves as the proper methods of dealing with criminals. We have to treat them physically as sick people, which in every respect they are. It is no more reasonable to punish these individuals for behaviour over which they have no control than it is to punish an individual for breathing through his mouth because of enlarged adenoids . . . It is the hope of the more progressive elements in psychopathology and criminology that the guard and the jailer will be replaced by the nurse, and the judge by the psychiatrists, whose sole attempt will be to treat and cure the individual instead of merely to punish him. Then and only then can we hope to lessen, even if not to entirely abolish, crime, the most costly burden that society has today.[2]

This is, however, the twentieth century approach, and even at that, it is not yet the basis of prison administration in every country of the world.

Let us briefly notice in this chapter and the next, how

the principles and purposes of prison administration have evolved from the ancient to the present days in India, Europe and America.

Administration of Justice in Ancient India

In ancient India at the time of the *Arthasastra*, justice was administered in accordance with legal rules which fell under one or the other of the following four heads : (a) Sacred Law (*Dharma*), (b) Secular Law (*Vyavahara*), (c) Custom (*Charitra*), and (d) Royal Commands (*Rajasasana*). "Sacred Law", says Chanakya, "is the embodiment of truth ; Secular Law depends upon evidence ; Custom is decided by the opinion of people ; and Royal Edicts constitute administrative law."[3] Of all these four divisions of law, customs were the most popular, and Manu and all other law-givers of that time accepted it as the essential principle in the administration of justice that disputes should be decided in accordance with the customs of the countries and districts (*janapada*), of castes (*jati*), and guilds (*sreni*), and of families (*kula*).[4]

But whatever be the legal rules for the administration of justice or whatever importance attached to any one of the different sets of legal rules, the King in ancient Indian society was the fountain of justice and the punishment of offenders was considered to be his sacred duty. And it is for this reason that the King in those days was called *Dandadhara*, 'the holder of Danda', i.e., the power of punishment or an incarnation of the *Yama*, the judge of the souls of the dead. It was then strongly felt that "if the King ceases to punish the subjects who swerve from the path of duty, the whole world will be destroyed, . . . the *Sudras* will rule the world and the strong will roast the weak on the spit like fish. The punishment is identical with *Dharma* ; it is the dark, red-eyed God, the son of the creator of the world under whose mighty rule the world feels itself secure. Punishment protects mankind and keeps watch when mankind sleep. The whole world is held in order by means of punishment, for a faultless man is very rare ; even the gods and demigods are driven to perform their duty by fear of punishment."[5]

With this idea of the utility and necessity of punishment,

the law-givers of ancient India prescribed severe punishments for crimes. In civil actions the usual remedies given by the courts were restoration of property and fines. In criminal cases the punishments were : (i) fine, (ii) imprisonment, (iii) whipping, (iv) physical torture, (v) banishment, (vi) condemnation to work in the mines, and (vii) death.[6] Barbarous punishments such as mutilation of limbs and detracting punishments such as riding on an ass, sprinkling of urine and shaving of the head, etc. were also provided for criminal offences. The brutal forms of punishments were beheading, drowning, burning, roasting, impaling, cutting into pieces, trampling down by wild elephants, tearing to pieces by dogs, etc. "In the case of mutilation and execution, as in other ancient systems of punishment, the principle of retaliation (Talion) as well as symbolical punishments come into play. The offender or the robber shall lose that limb with which he assaults or injures anybody . . . Moreover, the brand-marking of the drinker with the flag of a tavern and of the incestuous person with the mark of feminine pudendum were also symbolical."[7] Detracting punishments, mentioned above, were no less symbolical in character.

Despite such severe and brutal punishments prescribed by the law-givers, we find from the historical accounts left by foreign travellers that the extreme penalty of death and any other kind of corporal punishment were rarely inflicted by the rulers in ancient India. "The King", says Fa Hien, "in the administration of justice inflicts no corporal punishment, but each culprit is fined in money according to the gravity of his offence, and even in cases where the culprit has been guilty of repeated attempts to excite rebellion, they restrict themselves to the cutting off his right hand." Hiuen Tsiang and Sung Yun also confirmed this statement. Hiuen Tsiang, for instance, says : "There is no infliction of corporal punishment ; they are simply left to live or die, and are not counted among men". Megasthenes refers to cropping of the hair as a punishment. "If one is guilty", says he, "of a heinous offence, the King orders his hair to be cropped, this being a punishment in the last degree infamous."[8]

However, as castism conditioned and controlled every

aspect of an individual's life in the Hindu society of ancient India, the administration of legal justice was entirely coloured by it. The status of both the offender and the victim in the cast hierarchy was the basic criterion for the award of punishment for an offence. In case of theft, for instance, the Brahmin remained unpunished if he took away the property of his *Sudra* slave. Stealing gold from a Brahmin. on the other hand, was considered to be an offence punishable by death.[9] Commenting on this outstanding feature of the administration of legal justice in earlier Hindu society, an eminent researcher on ancient Indian history writes : "Although every member of the society had a *locus standi* in the courts, the idea of equality before the law was not fully developed in ancient India. A modified form of privilege ran through the whole system of Hindu Jurisprudence. The law was not the same for all, but depended upon the status of the person concerned."[10]

Another interesting feature of the administration of legal justice in ancient India is that the offenders in most cases were allowed to pay fines to escape punishments. In the *Smrtis*, for instance, fines are most frequently mentioned in connection with the rules of punishment.[11] In Kautilya's *Arthasastra* there is a separate chapter titled 'Fines in Lieu of Mutilation of Limbs'. Hiuen Tsiang also said that in India the usually inflicted punishments were life-long imprisonment, especially in the case of rebels, mutilation of nose, ears, hands, feet, banishment and ransom, and the money equivalent frequently paid to escape punishment.[12] Even in the case of murder, the offender could avoid capital punishment by paying the blood-money, i.e., the price of blood. Julius Jolly, referring to other writers on ancient Hindu law and custom, has observed that the penal laws of the *Smrtis*, in spite of their agreement with the principle of state justice, have preserved the traces of a state of things when the atonement for murder and slaughter was still regarded as a private affair and when the blood-money used to be paid.[13]

Of all the ancient punishments mentioned so far, punishment by imprisonment was very uncommon and in the ancient works, this type of punishment is rather rarely mentioned.[14]

It simply implies that the principal purpose of prison administration in ancient India was the detention of offenders awaiting trial or execution of sentence. Another purpose, albeit secondary, was to deter others from committing crime by exposing the prisoners to public gaze for which Manu (9,288) suggests that the prison-houses should be built on public roads so that everybody could see the suffering and disfigured criminals, who, as the commentaries elucidate it, with their body emaciated with hunger and thurst, disordered hair and beard, sometimes fettered in chains and mutilated, would produce a horrible impression on the onlookers.[15]

Penal System in Mughal India

The cruel and barbarous penal system of the ancient days continued for quite a long time in our country until the downfall of the Mughal Empire. Under the judicial system of the Mughals, the only law recognized in the country was the *Quranic* law which too prescribed brutal punishments for crimes. The *Quranic* law had originated and developed outside India, viz., in Arabia and Egypt, the chief centres of Islamic thought and culture. The orthodox Mughal Emperors and their judges instead of supplementing or adding any new principle or rule to this law, accepted it as it was interpreted by eminent Muslim jurists of the past. Thus, "Muslim Law in India", as a well-known Indian historian, Sir Jadunath Sarkar, aptly remarked, "was incapable of growth and change, except so far as it reflected changes of juristic thought in Arabia and Egypt".[16] No wonder then, our penal system remained cruel and barbarous during the long reign of the Mughals in India.

The punishments for crimes prescribed by the Islamic law were of four classes : (1) *hadd*, (2) *tazir*, (3) *quisas* and (4) *tashir*.

Hadd is a punishment unambiguously prescribed by Common Law and considered as 'the right of God' which no human judge can alter. The purpose of this punishment is to deter others from committing similar offence. The forms of punishment in this category included stoning to death for adultery, scourging for drinking wine and other intoxicant liquors, cutting off the right hand for theft, death either by the sword or by being impaled for robbery with murder, etc.

Tazir is a punishment intended to reform the criminal and inflicted for such crimes as have no *hadd* punishment. It was not 'the right of God'. On the contrary, its severity and magnitude were left entirely to the discretion of the judges for which attempts were often made to escape this type of punishment by bribery. It could take one of these four forms :

(i) *Tadib*, or public reprimand.
(ii) *Jirr*, or dragging the offender to the door (of the court house ?) and exposing him to public scorn ; somewhat like putting a man in the pillory.
(iii) Imprisonment or exile.
(iv) Boxing on the ear ; scourging.

Qusas or retaliation rested on the personal right of the victim or his next of kin, in the case of certain types of crimes such as a murder. He could either demand the legal punishment or accept the money damages, i.e. 'price of blood' offered by the murderer or pardon him unconditionally as he wished. It was exclusively his personal right and neither the *qazi* nor the king was to take any further notice of the crime. For minor offences, the retaliation was like the Mosaic law, 'a tooth for a tooth and an eye for an eye', with certain exceptions.

Tash-hir or public degradation was a popularly-devised punishment of universal currency throughout the Muslim world and even Hindu India and Medieval Europe. It included such punishments as shaving off the offender's head, making him ride on an ass with his face turned towards its tail, and his body covered with dust, sometimes with a garland of old shoes placed around his neck ; parading him in this posture through the streets with noisy music and finally turning him out of the city. It is neither recognized nor condemned in the law-books of Islam, but has been inflicted by all Muslim *qazis* and kings, and even by the lay public.

As for the offences against the state, such as rebellion, peculation and default in the payment of revenue, the *Quranic* law is silent and as such the sovereign was the sole authority in inflicting punishment in such cases.

The capital punishment or *qatl* was inflicted in certain cases of immorality, highway robbery, and apostasy (*murtadd*) from Islam, etc. Among the prevalent forms of execution were tampling down the offender by infuriated elephants, burying him alive, causing him to be stung to death by cobras or pressing him to death, the last being also sanctioned by medieval English law.[17]

During the Muslim rule in India punishment by imprsionment was not as uncommon as in ancient Hindu India. However, it was not so widely used as in British India. "There were two kinds of prisons, one for prisoners of high rank and the other for ordinary criminals. Important nobles and princes guilty of treason and rebellion were imprisoned in the fortresses situated in different parts of the country, the prominant among them being those at Gwalior, Ranthambhor, Rhotas, Bhakkar and Bayana. There were jails at the capital and at the headquarters of the provinces, districts and parganas. Besides regular prisoners, undertrials were also kept confined in jails."[18] Thus, in Muslim India since prisons were used both for detention and punishment of offenders the purpose of prison administration was not merely to keep the accused persons under safe custody but also to administer prisons as a means for punishing convicted criminals.

Growth of Modern Prison System under the British Rule

The prison system as it operates today in our country is a legacy of the British rule. It was an ingenious creation of the colonial rulers over our indigenous penal system with the prime motive of making imprisonment "a terror to wrongdoers". Nevertheless, it was a great leap in the history of our penal reforms as it facilitated the abolition of our antediluvian system of barbarous punishments and substitution of imprisonment as the chief form of punishment for the commission of crimes. The following extracts from the historic Minute of Lord Macaulay issued at a meeting of the Legislative Council of India on December 21, 1835 is a reflection of this observation :

> It is scarcely necessary to say that the best criminal code can be of very little use to a community, unless there be a good machinery for the infliction of punishment. Death is rarely inflicted in this country at present, and it must certainly be the wish of the Government and of the Law Commission that it should be inflicted more rarely still. The practice of (public) flogging has been abolished, and we should, I am sure, be most unwilling to revive it . Imprisonment is the punishment to which we must chiefly trust. It will probably be resorted to in ninety nine cases out of every hundred.[19]

It was quite natural that the early British administration had formulated its prison policy with a view to serving its colonial interests alone. "The East India Company", as Dr. B.K. Bhattacharya has very aptly observed, "believed only in keeping in custody the prisoners as economically as possible and with the maximum *profit* to the Government. Considering the state of prisons in England itself in those days, it is not surprising that the utmost indifference, neglect and cruelty would mark the administration of jails through the District Magistrates."[20] As has been pointed out, it was Lord Macaulay who, for the first time in 1835, drew the attention of the Legislative Council of India to the deplorable conditions of the Indian jails and proposed to appoint a committee "for the purpose of collecting information as to the state of Indian prison and of preparing an improved plan of prison discipline . . . and to suggest such reforms as may make the place (the Jail at Alipore) a model for other prisons". The Council accepted Macaulay's proposal and appointed 'The Prison Discipline Committee' with Hon'ble H. Shakespeare as President and Lord Macaulay as one of the members. The report of the Committee came out in 1838.

The Prison Discipline Committee of 1836-38 directed for the first time the attention of the English rulers of India to various vices of the administration of Indian jails in those days, viz., the corruption of the subordinate establishment, the laxity of discipline and the system of employing the prisoners in extramural labour on the public roads, "without exception the worst method of treatment that has been provided under the British Government for this class of persons." But the Committee itself was not free from the enduring influence of these vices. Its views and observations "unmistakably reflect the attitude of the English rulers of our country in the second quarter of the nineteenth century. It was an attitude of remorseless, retributive justice to all law-breakers and they made no secret of it."[21] On the primary object of punishment, the views of the Committee will be apparent from the following extracts: "The great end of punishment is, according to our view, to *deter* all men from crime who are capable of committing it, and susceptible of the fear of punishment. We include the sufferer himself amongst those for whom this end is sought, whenever it is desirable to deter him from a repetition of his crime; and on this understanding it appears to us that this single object of punishment is of such paramount importance, that no secondary object ought to be aimed at in any such way that thereby this main object will be attained in any material degree less perfectly than would otherwise be the case."[22]

No wonder that the Committee of 1836-38 which expressed this view on the end of punishment, "deliberately rejected all such reforming influences as moral and religious teaching, education or any system of rewards for good conduct", "threw the whole weight of its authority in favour of increased rigour of treatment", and proposed to engage all convicts "in some dull, monotonous, wearisome and uninteresting task in which there shall be wanting even the enjoyment of knowing that a quicker release can be got by working harder for a time." The purpose of prison administration, as viewed in its Report, was to make "the Gaol a place of dread" through a ruthless process of "severe privation, really hard work, solitude, silence and separation." Notwithstanding its advocacy of the theory of retribution in prison administration, the Prison Discipline Committee of 1836-38 had still made some positive contributions in the sphere of prison reforms in this country. "Its advocacy of proper buildings and intramural employment", as the Indian Jails Committee of 1919-20, while giving an outline of the history of Indian prison reforms in its Report, has aptly remarked, "laid the foundation for further progress, and its vigorous grasp of principle placed the subject of prison reform in India on a higher plane than might otherwise have been at once attained."[23]

During the long period of over eighty years that elapsed since the Report of the Prison Discipline Committee came out in 1838, several commissions and committees were appointed by the British Government to go into the various aspects of prison management and discipline in this country. As a follow up of the recommendations made by these official bodies, various Prison Acts and Regulations were enacted including the Prisons Act of 1894 which is the current law governing administration of prisons in India. Since these efforts were confined to the *material* side of prison administration, the Indian jails appeared to have achieved considerable material progress during this period. Buildings had been gradually provided, dietaries laid down, systems of labour elaborated, a rational remission system developed, insanitary conditions partly corrected and death rates reduced.[24] Despite such material progress, the jail administration in India still lagged on its *reformative* side. The influence of the Report of the Prison Discipline Committee of 1836-38 was not yet completely eliminated. It still "cast its long shadow over the dull, bleak and cheerless Indian prisons and retarded all serious attempts at reform. The administrators were still in no mood to regard the prisoner as a human being and seek to reform him by humane methods, as opposed to methods of torture of either body or mind. He was looked upon as a mere cog in the jail wheel that turned on and on so ruthlessly. All emphasis was given to the material well-being of a prisoner—his diet, health and labour—totally ignoring the possibility of his moral or intellectual reclamation."[25] No wonder that the Indian jails, at this stage, could not exercise any "healthy influence" on their inmates. On the contrary, they "tend to harden if not to degrade" them and most men came out of prison worse than they went in.

Meanwhile, the science of prison administration made great advances in the West. The origin and causes of crime began to be studied in a 'new light'. New experiments in prison management were carried out. New strategies and techniques were evolved for prevention of crime and scientific treatment of criminals. The progressive thinkers of the West realized for the first time that inhuman handling of prisoners failed miserably to rehabilitate the criminals in society after release and accepted reformation of criminals as one of the primary objects of prison administration. America took the leadership in the application of these new methods of preventing crimes and dealing with offenders and inspired other western countries in the same direction. From the West, the "new light" gradually spread to other parts of the world.

In our country too, the British Government appointed a joint commission of officials and non-officials in 1919 "to investigate the whole subject of jail administration and to suggest improvements in the light of experience of the West." The result was the publication of the voluminous Indian Jails Committee Report of 1919-20. "It was an outstanding contribution to Indian prison administration and still remains an important landmaık in our journey towards the most modern penological reforms in this country."[26] "For India its practical importance", according to Dr. B.K. Bhattacharya, "is as great as that of the Gladstone Report in the history of English penal reforms."[27]

As regards the general objectives of prison administration, the Report of the Committee of 1919-20 observed : "there is very general agreement that crime is an anti-social act and that it is the task of the prison administrator so to deal with the offender that he and others may be *deterred* from the commission of such acts in future. It is also generally admitted by modern authorities that the aim of the prison administration should *further* be to effect such a *reformation* in the character of the criminal as will fit him again to take his place in society and to become a useful citizen. Whatever differences exist as to the methods to be employed, we take it that most penologists agree as to the objects in view, namely, the prevention of further crime and the restoration of the criminal to society as a reformed character."[28]

For the fulfilment of the objectives, mentioned above, the Committee of 1919-20 recommended *inter alia* the following measures as the essentials of prison administration :

1. As far as possible, every prison should be under the superintendence of a trained expert who should devote his whole time and attention to the subject, and the number of prisoners who can properly be entrusted to the care of a single superintendent must not exceed a certain maximum.
2. The prison staff, from the jailor down to the warder, should be recruited with care, properly trained and paid a salary sufficient to secure and retain faithful service.
3. Prisoners in jail shall be so classified and separated that the younger or less experienced shall not be contaminated or rendered worse by communication and association with the older or more hardened offender.
4. The prisoners, while in prison, should be brought under such humanizing and improving influences as will not only deter them from committing further crimes but will also result in a real reformation of their character.
5. It is desirable, as far as practicable, to help such prisoners as may need help on their release from prison, so that they may be given a reasonable chance of securing an honest living.
6. Since imprisonment is generally an evil, measures such as extension of the probation system, prohibition of petty sentences of imprisonment, extension of the period for payment of fine in reasonable cases as determined by the court and the practice of payment by instalments should be adopted as far as possible.
7. Measures for revision of every sentence of long imprisonment and grant of increased remission for good behaviour should be taken to shorten imprisonment.[29]

It goes without saying that by recommending these valuable measures for prison reform, the Indian Jails Committee of 1919-20 gave an impetus to modernization of jail administration in this country. In practice, however, not much had been done by the alien governments on the reformative side of prison system during the next quarter of a century that ended with the transfer of power to Indian hands in 1947. A correct appraisal of prison reforms under the British rule in India can be ascertained from the following observation of Shri R.G. Salvi in his inaugural address as a Convenor of the All India Jail Manual Committee of 1957-59 :

> Without being cynical or critical I may mention here that it is my feeling that whatever prison reforms have been introduced in Indian Prisons they have only been piecemeal. These reforms on the whole are nothing more than granting a few amenities and facilities to prisoners. These prison reforms can thus be termed as reforming conditions of living in prisons, rather than reforms to help the rehabilitation of the prisoner in society."[30]

Post-independence Developments in Indian Prison Administration

After the advent of freedom, a new phase of humanitarian prison administration has begun in India. Ideas regarding punishment and functions of prisons have been changing. A new awareness of the problem of crime and proper treatment of offenders has grown so much so that prison administration has off and on been subjected to severe criticism from the press, the Parliament and the judiciary. "Overcrowding in prisons, prolonged detention of undertrial prisoners, unsatisfactory living conditions, lack of treatment programmes and allegations of indifferent and even inhuman approach of prison staff have repeatedly attracted the attention of the critics over the years."[31] The changing circumstances on the socio-economic scene of the country after independence had also inspired a few conscientious prison administrators of our country to undertake some innovative experiments through their own individual efforts. Since such efforts and innovations were only sporadic and short lived, their total impact on prison administration was not discernible up to any appreciable extent.[32] As a matter of fact, no meaningful prison reforms can ever be made without the requisite political will. "As an old and experienced prisoner", says Mahatma Gandhi, "I believe that Governments have to begin the reform . . .Humanitarians can but supplement government efforts. As it is, the humanitarian, if he attempted anything, will first have to undo the mischief done in prisons where the environment hardens the criminal tendency, and in the case of innocent prisoners they learn how to commit crimes without being detected. I hold that humanitarian effort cannot cope with the evil wrought in the jails."[33] In order to have a correct view on the progress of prison reforms in independent India it is, therefore, extremely necessary to take stock of official efforts at bringing about changes in prison administration during the post-Independence period.

In the Constitution of Republic India prison administration has been included in the State List.[34] As prison rules and regulations vary from one State to another, the much-needed coordination is lacking. However, it was realized soon after independence that the Jail Manuals of the States of the Union, based on the antediluvian Prisons Act of 1894, could not cope with the new ideas and awareness of crime, criminals and their treatment that had been growing fast in the country. It was felt very strongly that whatever had prison reforms been made by our alien rulers were only sporadic and neither organically conceived nor uniform and hence, some broad guidelines should be given from the Centre with a view to coordinating the prison-reform programmes of the different State Governments.

The decade 1951-60 that followed immediately after Independence was a decade of enthusiasm for prison reforms. While local committees were being appointed by some State Governments (viz., Madras, Orissa, Uttar Pradesh and Maharashtra) to suggest prison reforms, the Government of India invited technical assistance in the field from the United Nations. Dr. Walter C. Reckless, a leading American criminologist, visited India as an U.N. expert during the years 1951-52 to suggest ways and means of prison reforms in the country. His report 'Jail Administration in India' is another landmark in our history of prison reforms. He made a plea for transforming jails into reformation centres and advocated establishment of new jails to perform specialized functions. He recommended, *inter alia*, a number of other important measures. viz., the getting out of juvenile delinquents from adult jails, courts and police lock-ups, specialized training programmes for correctional personnel of different ranks, the introduction of legal substitutes for short sentences, the development of whole-time probation and aftercare services, the setting up of revising boards for the selection of prisoners for premature release, the establishment of an Advisory Bureau for Correctional Administration at the Centre to help the State Governments in development of correctional programmes, holding of periodical conferences of the superior staff members of correctional departments and revision of outdated State Jail Manuals. The year 1952 further witnessed a break-through in national coordination on correctional work as in that year the Eighth Conference of the Inspectors General of Prisons was held after lapse of seventeen years. The Conference held at Bombay reiterated the need for revision of State Jail Manuals. The first open prisons were set up about this time in Uttar Pradesh and some other States and Prison Welfare Officers were appointed in a number of States in later years. A few new ideas of prison reforms were introduced in the country during this decade. The prisoners could now avail of furlough and parole. They were granted wages, albeit nominal, for the work done by them. The introduction of Panchayat system led to some improvement in the living conditions of prisoners. Jail Training Schools were set up in some States. Whipping was abolished in 1955 and the Probation of Offenders Act was enacted in 1958.[35]

Meanwhile, the United Nations held its First Congress on the Prevention of Crime and Treatment of Offenders at Geneva in 1955. The Congress approved the U.N. Standard Minimum Rules for the Treatment of Prisoners and urged the Member Nations to modify their national practices accordingly.

In 1957, the Government of India appointed the All India Jail Manual Committee for (i) preparing an All India Skeleton Jail Manual, (ii) examining the Prisons Act and other relevant Central laws and suggesting any necessary Central legislation, and (iii) making proposals for prison reforms to be adopted uniformly throughout the country. In order that the problems peculiar to different parts of the country and the need of coordination by the Centre might be given due emphasis, the All India Jail Manual Committee was constituted, among others, with the then Inspectors General of Prisons of Bombay, Madras, West Bengal, Uttar Pradesh, Punjab and Kerala.

This Committee of 1957-59 studied the problems of crime and delinquency from a very progressive angle and poignantly observed that the solutions to these problems do not lie only in prisons but in the larger socio-economic fields as well. In its view, these problems "can be solved neither by making punishment more deterrent nor by making the system of punishment too weak and diluted." Realizing the significance of Mahatma Gandhi's dictum that "criminals should be treated as patients in hospitals and jails should be hospitals admitting such patients for treatment and cure",[36] the Committee wanted prisons to be transformed into correctional institutions. Its view on the principal purpose of correctional administration is reflected in one of the assumptions it made while framing the Manual : "The primary objective of punishment is reclamation and rehabilitation of the offender and this objective will be faithfully implemented in correctional institutions."[37] In consonance with its radical approach to the problems of crime and delinquency and to the prime objective of correctional administration, the All India Jail Manual Committee furnished a detailed report containing necessary principles for modernization of prisons together with a Model Prison Manual in 1960 as a broad guideline for the States to revise their outdated Prison Manuals.

Another major post-Independence development in the Indian prison administration was the setting up of the Central Bureau of Correctional Services in 1961 as a central technical advisory body with the broad objectives of evolving modern policies and programmes in social defence field, collection of factual data and statistics, exchange of information, professional training, empirical research studies and publications. The Bureau functioned under the Government of India's Ministry of Home Affairs until 1964 when it was transferred to the newly created Department of Social Security, now known as the Ministry of Social Welfare. It was reconstituted in 1975 as the National Institute of Social Defence and its functions were enlarged to include preventive, correctional and rehabilitative aspects of social defence, viz., welfare of prisoners, prison reforms/administration, juvenile vagrancy, probation, beggary, social and moral hygiene, alcoholism, gambling, drug addiction, etc. The Institute continues to work under the Ministry of Social Welfare and has been playing "a useful role" in its enlarged field of social defence.[38] However, there are still certain important areas of activity such as compilation of all-India statistics on prisons, probation and parole, where the Institute has not been able to play its due role for reasons beyond its control, viz., lack of cooperation from some of the State Governments.

Unfortunately, some sporadic achievements apart, the spirit and enthusiasm with which the task of prison reforms was taken up by the Central and some State Governments during the decade 1951-60 did not last long. The valuable recommendations of the Committees appointed by these Governments were not implemented in an effective manner. Official apathy and bureaucratic bungling continued so much so that even after the end of another decade (1961-70) the general state of prison administration in the country was described by an official committee as "depressing". In 1972, the Government of India's Ministry of Home Affairs appointed a Working Group on Prisons for (i) examining the physical and administrative conditions of the jails in the country and suggesting ways and means of their improvement ; (ii) laying down standards in respect of different services and facilities in the jails ; (iii) laying down an order of priorities for the prison development schemes and (iv) considering other allied matters concerning prisons and prisoners. A year later, the Group submitted its report in which it emphasized the need for a National Policy on Prison and Correctional Administration. Discarding the traditional prison-based policy, the report of the Group identified the main elements of the proposed National Policy, the more important of them being as follows :

1. A suitable system should be established for coordination among the three organs of the criminal justice system, i.e., the police, the judiciary and the prison and correctional administration, for the effective prevention of crime and treatment of offenders.

2. The supreme aim of punishment has now to be the protection of society through the rehabilitation of offender. The reassimilation of the offender in society and the prevention of crime are now the principal goals for the criminal justice system. Accordingly, the aim of the prison administration will be the employment of all resources, human and material, to provide scientific treatment to every offender according to his peculiar needs and circumstances.
3. The concepts of deprivation of liberty and segregation from society should be limited mostly to the habitual, the incorrigible and the dangerous criminals and the Government should make fullest possible use of various alternatives to imprisonment as a measure of sentencing policy. Non-institutional and semi-institutional forms of treatment should be resorted to as far as possible.
4. There should be close coordination between the prison and the probation and other correctional services. It follows that the prison administration should be treated as an integral part of the social defence component of the national planning process.
5. Free legal aid should be provided to all indigent prisoners.
6. Undertrial prisoners should be lodged in separate institutions as far as possible and facilities should be provided to them for work on a voluntary basis.
7. The Union and State Governments should declare unequivocally that there will be no bar or restriction on the employment of ex-convicts of specified categories in the public services after a due scrutiny of the prison reports certifying to their abilities and qualities.
8. The prison administration should systematically involve enlightened individual citizens, associations, societies and other community agencies in the treatment, aftercare and rehabilitation of offenders.[39]

In order to usher in the desired changes in the prison administration as a whole, the Group recommended that the highest priority should be given to the adoption of the National Policy on Prisons as suggested by them along with the inclusion of certain aspects of the prison administration in the Five Year Plan, the amendment of the Constitution to include the subject of prisons and allied institutions in the Concurrent List, the enactment of suitable legislation by the Centre as well as the States, and the revision of the State Prison Manuals.[40]

While the report of the Working Group was gathering dust, the Government of India requested the Seventh Finance Commission to go into the question of upgrading the standards of jail administration on the basis of a comprehensive assessment of the requirements in this regard. The Commission in its report of 1978 based on an analysis of the data collected from various sources at national and regional levels, admitted that jails had been neglected for too long and that there had been practically no improvement in their environments or in the methods of dealing with inmates. The Commission recommended that priority should be given : firstly, to ensure that adequate direct expenditure was incurred on the prisoners; secondly, to bring improvements in amenities in respect of water supply, sanitary facilities, electrification, etc. and, thirdly, to provide for the construction of additional jail capacities in States where these were found short of the minimum requirements. It considered necessary that a norm of Rs. 3 per head for diet and Re. 1 per day per prisoner for other items like medicine, clothing, etc. should be a minimum, and that inclusive of prison overheads (but excluding the headquarters cost of direction and administration) a minimum of Rs. 6 per day per prisoner should be provided for in all the States. Accordingly, the Commission recommended an allocation of Rs. 48.31 crores for the States which were found backward in these respects.[41]

While the planning and monitoring of the schemes recommended by the Seventh Finance Commission were being assigned to the National Institute of Social Defence through the Ministry of Home Affairs, the Government of India appointed another Committee (the All India Committee on Jail Reforms) in July 1980 for making a comprehensive review of prison administration in the country and suggesting suitable measures for its improvement. Headed by Justice Anand Narain Mulla, the Committee submitted its report in 1983. It noted with profound regret that the United Nations Standard Minimum Rules for the Treatment of Prisoners were not being generally observed in several States and Union Territories in India and that the conditions of prisons in the country had been deteriorating and had reached a point of crisis. One of the main reasons for this general deterioration, according to the Committee, was the lack of national commitment arising out of a national consensus on the goals and objectives of prison administration and modalities of achieving them. The Committee had, therefore, formulated the draft of a National Policy on Prisons (see Appendix) and recommended for its adoption by the Government of India in consultation with the State Governments and Union Territory Administrations. The goals and objectives of prisons in India, according to the proposed National Policy on Prisons, are to protect society and to reform and reassimilate offenders in the social milieu by giving them appropriate correctional treatment. The modalities of achieving these goals and objectives have been clearly laid down in it. The Committee, however, feels that crime being a social problem cannot be tackled merely through legislation or pronouncement of laudable objectives. "Unless a large section of the society believes in the reformative and rehabilitative approaches", observes the Committee, "a progressive and modern system of prisons cannot become a reality."[42] It therefore recommends very aptly that a regular plan aiming at creating a favourable *rehabilitation culture* in the society should be drawn up and implemented by the prison administration. It remains to be observed whether these valuable recommendations will be implemented by the Governments or whether official apathy and bureaucratic bungling will continue unabated in "cynical disregard" of social interest.

The foregoing study clearly reveals that our policy makers do not lack theoretical awareness of the objectives and principles of modern prison administration. What really lacking are the political and administrative will and initiative to bring about the desired reforms in conformity with the acquired knowledge. Little wonder that in most of the States and Union Territories official efforts at prison reforms have so far been confined primarily to the appointment of commissions or committees without implementing their valuable recommendations. In West Bengal, for instance, three such committees were appointed between 1969 and 1978 with the identical object of revising the antediluvian Jail Code inherited from the British. The first Committee, constituted by the United Front Ministry in 1969 with Shri Prasanta Sur as Chairman, worked for about a year and a half but could not submit any report. The next one, headed by Shri Sukhomoy Dutt, was appointed by the Congress Ministry in 1972. This Committee suggested many liberal, meaningful and practical reforms. Surprisingly enough, instead of taking any follow-up action on these recommendations, the first Left Front Ministry preferred to appoint yet another Committee in 1978. Headed by Shri Tarapada Lahiri it submitted its report in late 1980. That report, too, is still gathering dust.

Thus, nearly four decades after freedom, the ghost of the British Raj still haunts our prisons much more than any other government institution. The existing physical and administrative conditions of the jails throughout the country are not at all conducive to reformative treatment. While much-needed reforms are pending, our prisons continue to serve as breeding places for hardened criminals rather than the correctional institutions they should be. Paucity of funds, of course, stand in the way. But the fact remains that many meaningful reforms could have been achieved even under the prevailing financial constraints if political will and initiative were there.[43]

It must be interesting in this connection to discuss in brief the evolution of the purposes and principles of prison administration in other parts of the world, particulary in Europe and America, and this we shall do in the next chapter.

NOTES AND REFERENCES

1. Edwin H. Sutherland and Donald R. Cressey, *Principles of Criminology*, Sixth edn., 2nd Indian Reprint, 1968, p. 310.
2. Benjamin Karpman, "Criminality, Insanity, and the Law," *Journal of*

Criminal Law and Criminology (Northwestern University School of Law), 39 : 584-605, January—February, 1949 ; See also Sutherland and Cressey, *op .cit.*, p. 311.

3. *Arthasastra*, Book III, Chap. 1 ; See also Pramathanath Banerjee, *Public Administration in Ancient India*, 1916, pp. 149-50.
4. Banerjee, *op. cit.*, p. 151.
5. Manu—7, 14-30 ; Vishnu—3, 95 ; Yajnavalkya—1,356-56; Narada—I 1, 1 etc. ; See also Julius Jolly, Tr. Batakrishna Ghosh, *Hindu Lāw and Custom*, 1928, p. 280.
6. Banerjee, *op. cit.*, p. 166.
7. Jolly, Tr. Ghosh, *op. cit.*, pp. 281-82.
8. Fa Hien (Beal)—Chap. XVI ; Buddihist Records (Beal)—Book II ; Megasthenes—Fragment—XXVII. D. ; See also Banerjee, *op. cit.*, pp. 166-67.
9. Manu—8, 417 ; 8, 337f etc. ; See also Jolly, Tr. Ghosh, *op. cit.*, pp. 273-74.
10. Banerjee, *op. cit.*, pp. 170-71.
11. Jolly, Tr. Ghosh, *op. cit.*, p. 281.
12. *Ibid.*, p. 283.
13. *Ibid.*, p. 284.
14. *Ibid.*, p. 282.
15. *Ibid.*, p. 282.
16. Jadunath Sarkar, *Mughal Administration*, 4th edn., 1952, p. 101.
17. *Ibid.*, pp. 103-07.
18. A.L Srivastava, *The History of India* : 1000 A.D.—1707 A.D., Ist edn., 1964, p. 522. This statement relating to the operation of prisons during the reign of Akbar the Great may enable us to understand the general purposes of prisons under the Muslim rule in India for, the purposes of prison administration during the reign of other Mughal Emperors were not very different from what has been indicated here.
19. Govt. of India : National Archives of India—Documents connected with Prisons Act, 1894 : Legislative Department Proceedings No. 164 to 271.
20. B.K. Bhattacharya, in Itallies, 1958, p. 3.
21. Govt. of West Bengal : Report of the Jail Code Revision Committee, 1972-73, p. 8.
22. Report of the Prison Discipline Committee, 1836-38, para 228.
23. Report of the Indian Jails Committee, 1919-20, para 9.
24. *Ibid.* para 13.
25. Govt. of West Bengal, Report of the Jail Code Revision Committee, p. 10.
26. *Ibid.*
27. Bhattacharya, *op. cit.*, p. 4.
28. *Supra.* note 23 at para 15.
29. *Supra.* note 23 at paras 16-20.

30. Report of the All India Jail Manual Committee, 1957-59, Annexure IA, p. 129.
31. Govt. of India : Ministry of Home Affairs, Report of the All India Committee on Jail Reforms, 1980-83, p. 1.
32. *Ibid.*, p. 11.
33. *Young India*, February 19, 1926.
34. Item No. 4 in List II (State List) in the Seventh Schedule of the Constitution.
35. Vide Report of the Working Group on Prisons in the Country, 1972-73 and Report of the All India Committee on Jail Reforms, 1980-83.
36. Quoted, Report of the All India Jail Manual Committee, 1957-59, para 3.
37. *Ibid.*, para 20.
38. *Supra.*, note 31 at p. 337.
39. Govt. of India : Ministry of Home Affairs, Report of the Working Group on Prisons in the Country, 1972-73, pp. 20-24.
40. *Ibid.*, pp. 143-44.
41. *Supra.* note 31 at pp. 15-16.
42. *Supra.* note 31 at pp. 25-26.
43. For further details see, Jaytilak Guha Roy, "Cleansing of the Jails," *The Statesman*, Calcutta, March 14, 1983.

2

PRISON ADMINISTRATION IN EUROPE AND AMERICA : HISTORICAL RESUME

In ancient Europe, as in India, punishments for the commission of crimes were meted out on the basis of retribution and for this, they were severe and barbarous. The usual modes of punishment were fines, physical torture, mutilation of limbs, public humiliation, banishment, branding and death. Each of these forms of punishment, as pointed out by Dr. Walter C. Reckless, had also several variations and applications. Death penalty, for instance, included hanging, crucifixion, burning at the stake, and so on. Physical torture and mutilation also assumed many forms as flogging, burning, disfiguration, dismemberment, and so on.[1]

The motive behind the infliction of severe and barbarous punishments was to frighten and deter others from the commission of similar crimes. John C. Ball in an article, makes this clear : "In antiquity torturous deaths and mutilations were exacted with the thought of making an example of the malefactor. It is for this reason that crucifixion was employed as a means of execution by the Romans".[2]

Many of the above-mentioned forms of punishment were symbolic in relation to the specific crime Gillin refers to these as poetic punishments and says : "Thus the thief often had his hand cut off. The false witness had his totngue torn out or pierced. The crime of rape was often punished by emasculation. The Baptists of Switzerland were punished by being drowned".[3]

Imprisonment as a form of punishment was by no means unknown but rarely used in ancient Europe and in Roman Law, at least, it was *forbidden*. As the Jurist Ulpian wrote : "Provincial governors usually sentence people to be held in prison or to be fettered. This is illegal, since such forms of punishment have been prohibited . . . Prisons ought to be used for detention only, but not for punishment."[4]

In ancient Europe imprisonment or confinement, therefore, "was normally a preliminary to the appropriate punishment, such as execution, banishment, a fine or to release of the prisoner after trial"[5] and "prisons were places of temporary housing to await the actual punishment decreed".[6] The primary objective of prison administration was nothing more than the detention of offenders awaiting trial or execution of sentence.

It seems to be quite clear then that in antiquity the European system of punishment was very much akin to the Indian system and consequently, there was hardly any difference in the primary objective of prison administration in both Europe and India in those days.

In the Middle Ages the ancient system of punishment continued in Europe and the penalty of imprisonment was either forbidden in law or rarely awarded. The ancient Roman idea that "prison ought to be used for detention only, but not for punishment" was an accepted legal principle in most of Europe in the Middle Ages, although, as in the days of Ulpian, it was not infrequently violated.[7] Even in the later Middle Ages, imprisonment as a penalty was either unknown or used only for very restricted groups of offenders. In France, for example, the last code of laws prior to the Revolution was enacted in 1670 and contained no mention of imprisonment as a penalty.[8] Even as late as 1771, the French Jurist Jousse stated that prison was used only to hold criminals before trial and not to punish them for their crimes.[9]

In Frankfort, on the other hand, it was ordered in the first part of the sixteenth century that for certain offences "the criminal shall be imprisoned and forgotten for a time". Nevertheless, imprisonment was sometimes used in France and other Western countries either as a means of securing the payment of fines or as a commutation of death penalty when mitigating circumstances were found.[10]

In medieval England, when Henry de Bracton wrote the first comprehensive treatise on English law, *De legibus et consuetudivibus Angliae*, he referred to prisons as places "where men remained only until it had been decided whether they should be punished or freed. Nevertheless, imprisonment as a form of punishment was somewhat commoner in England than on the Continent, where legal systems were based more closely on Roman Law".[11] Henry II, for instance, provided a penalty of imprisonment for one year for perjury in a grand assize ; Henry III provided the same penalty for breaches of the forest law ; and the Statute of Westminster of 1275 punished rape with two years' imprisonment.[12] Incarceration was also used in medieval England as a means of enforcing the payment of fines. In 1241, for example, some Jews convicted of circumcising a Christian child were ordered either to pay twenty thousand marks or else be kept perpetual prisoners.[13]

These few exceptions apart, "Medieval Anglo-Saxon society, with its wide use of capital and corporal punishment, had little use for imprisonment",[14] and even up to the middle of the twelfth century, "some counties (in England) were without public goals or prisoners' cages, and Henry II commanded their construction at the Assize of Claredon, 1166."[15] Confirming this Barnes and Teeters say : "As we understand the jail in more modern times, we might accept the date of origin as 1166, when Henry II commanded the construction of jails at the Assize of Claredon".[16] These jails were, in the beginning, administered under the 'fee system'. The sheriff and magistrates of the English counties did not assume any direct responsibility for the maintenance of the jails or for the treatment of their occupants. This "unpleasant chore" was turned over to the private keeper as a concession. The keepers were not paid any salary. Their income came from fees exacted from the prisoners or their friends and relatives. Naturally, the fees that they charged were so high as to enable them to operate prisons with profits. In these goals the "prisoners and their families were kept at their own expense for months or years awaiting the time of trial, well fed if they had means, but perhaps starved to death if they were poor. At a later date, the prisoners hung collecting bags out of their windows on Sunday mornings."[17] This 'fee system' continued in England for several centuries without much criticism in official circles until the time of the great prison reformer, John Howard.[18]

Imprisonment, however, came into extensive use in the later half of the thirteenth century during the reign of Edward I. But even in this period, it was used primarily as "squeezer" or means of securing fines.[19]

The foregoing discussion clearly reveals that the principal objective of jail administration in most of the European countries in the Middle Ages and even thereafter was only to detain the offenders awaiting trial or execution of sentence and to squeeze them for payment of their fines or debts which incidentally yielded good profits to the keepers of the jails.

After the collapse of feudalism, Western Europe in the sixteenth century was swarmed with paupers, mendicants and roving outlaws. Great numbers of the rural population who had been forced to leave their lands and estates and the mercenary armies and soldiers left by the feudal barons were all congregated in the towns and cities and created an acute socio-economic problem for the whole of Western Europe. It was to solve this that the city of London established a workhouse in 1557 in a former royal palace at Bridewell which was given to it for this purpose by Edward VI in 1553 under the influence of Sir Thomas Lever and Bishop Ridely. This was the first house of correction, and the term 'bridewell' came to be applied to other similar institutions that sprang up in England soon after. By an act of 1576, the British Parliament provided that every county should have a house of correction, and in 1609 such institution became mandatory in every English county.

Originally, the major purposes of the administration of these institutions were to correct idleness and vagrancy on the one hand, and to make profits on the other, by compelling sturdy beggars and vagabonds sent there to do hard and unpleasant work. Later, these institutions also came to be gradually used for imprisoning minor offenders. In 1630, by an order of the Privy Council, houses of correction were located next to the jails so that misdemeanants could be put to work instead of being confined idle in the jails. In 1711, by an Act of Parliament, the maximum term of imprisonment in these institutions was fixed at three years. By subsequent legislation, the number of offences for which persons might be confined was largely increased. And through this process, the English houses of correction gradually lost their original correctional function and became regular jails for convicted persons.[20]

However, the establishment of London's famous Bridewell in 1557 marked the beginning of a new era in the history of the evolution of the European penal institutions. It was an era "of experimentation with imprisonment as a form of *punishment* for certain types of offenders".[21] In other parts of Europe, houses of correction on the pattern of Bridewell were started by the Dutch. Possibly through the English influence they established a house of correction in Amsterdam in 1595[22] which, "based on the principle of compulsory work, but separated from poor relief, included vagrants, disorderly women, thieves, and neglected children".[23] The first spinning house for women and the first separate house for children were also founded in the same city in 1596 and 1600 respectively. Following the Dutch pattern, houses of correction were later established in Germany, Switzerland and many other countries on the continent of Europe. "Some authorities are inclined to accept the Amsterdam workhouses and the English Bridewells as the first prisons for sentenced offenders".[24]

The ultimate object of the administration of these establishments was the reformation of offenders. But unfortunately, *this noble end was sought to be fulfilled by wrong means of strict discipline of punishment and hard labour with little* touch of human sympathy. There was very little emphasis on the classification of inmates according to age, sex or other principles. The most striking feature was the deplorable conditions of these institutions which "soon produced wide-spread agitation for further changes in methods of handling criminals. Leading agitators included Montesquieu, Voltaire, Thomas Paine, Diderot, Adam Smith, Bentham, Sir Samuel Romilly, John Howard, and Elizabeth Fry. These leaders painstakingly exposed and publicized the conditions of filth and immorality that prevailed in these houses which, they charged, instead of reforming their inmates, actually fostered crime & disease . . ."[25]

The two institutions that, however, attracted much attention of these agitators and influenced the later dominant prison system in America and England were the Hospice of San Michele, a reformatory for boys established in Rome by Pope Clement XI in 1703 and the *Maison de Force*, a house of correction, opened by Jean Jacques Philippe Vilain (1717-77) in Ghent, Belgium in 1773. The former institution has been accepted by some leading authorities as the *first modern prison.* It was established on the monastic philosophy of expiation. Its principal purpose was moral regeneration of juvenile offenders through penitence and reflection in cellular isolation at night and congregate work under a strict rule of silence during the day. The incorrigible boys, however, were kept separated, day and night, in their little cells. The inmates were classified according to their age, nature and the gravity of their offence. Religious instruction was also provided for moral regeneration of offenders.

Vilain's institution at Ghent could be considered one of the first long-term convict prisons, for it initiated the famous octagonal plan of construction.[26] It also illustrates rudimentary classification of prisoners, because its varied inmates—felons, misdemeanants, vagrants and also women and children—were kept in separate sections. The primary purpose of this institution was to reform the criminals by engaging them not in unpleasant and unproductive occupations as was done earlier by its predecessor, the English Bridewells, but in productive trades. For the fulfilment of its primary purpose, it also followed the policy of cellular isolation of prisoners at night and congregate work in shops during the day.

These two institutions at Rome and Belgium were nothing more than examples of "a few isolated, historical predecessor" of the modern prison system and it was not until the early part of the nineteenth century that imprisonment came to be the normal method of punishing offenders in Europe, England and America. Before that, "capital punishment was decreed for hundreds of crimes, and when capital punishment was not resorted to, corporal punishment was the alternative ; hands and other appropriate appendages were lopped off. Offenders were pilloried and subjected to public degradation. In some situations, the property of the convict was confiscated and he was banished from the country to labour in frightful prison colonies."[27] In England, even in 1832, a nine-year old child was sentenced to death for smashing a window and stealing two-pence worth of paint and it was only in 1832 that two hundred offences hitherto punishable by death ceased to be capital crimes in that country.[28]

The grounds for the diminution of capital and corporal punishments as well as the practical beginning of imprisonment as a normal method of punishing offenders had been prepared, as Harry Barnes says, "by the moral revival led by Wesley and Whitfield, the humanitarianism of the French *philosophers*, and the English and American Quakers, and the progress of rational jurisprudence in the works of Montesquieu, Beccaria, Romilly and Bentham."[29] With the diminution of capital and corporal punishments in England, America and other Western countries, there was not only a very definite need for a prison where convicted persons could serve sentences but there was also a clamour among the progressive reformers, the most famous of whom being John Howard, for separate confinement of prisoners, to overcome the filth and vice of indiscriminate herding in most of the jails and prisons of the time.[30] Separate or solitary confinement also appealed to these reformers "because they believed that solitude would help the offender to become penitent and that penitence would result in reformation."[31] Thus evolved the penitentiary concept of imprisonment which soon dominated the European prison systems.

The concept of 'penitence' or 'penitentiary reformation, however, was not something new. The medieval ecclesiastical prisons of Europe had also this ideal. But it was John Howard (1726-90), the great English prison reformer, who deserves credit not only for popularizing this ideal but also for "sparking a general interest in the reformation of character" as a major purpose of prison administration. After his assumption of the post of High Sheriff of Bedfordshire in 1730, Howard paid an extensive visit to the English county jails. Being horrified by the deplorable conditions in those jails, he left England in April, 1775 for a series of visits to many of the prisons and workhouses in Europe. After collecting necessary data for more than a year, he returned home and devoted himself to the writing of his great work, 'The State of Prisons in England Wales, with Preliminary Observations, and an Account of Some Foreign Prisons', published in 1777. This classic in penology cast enormous influence on penal reform and prison administration both in Europe and America.

In Europe, Howard found deplorable abuses existing in the prisons. The two institutions that, however, attracted his attention were the Hospice of San Michele at Rome and the House of Correction at Ghent, as mentioned earlier. According to Barnes and Teeters, "It was the monastic philosophy of expiation dominating the Hospice that pleased John Howard most as he observed the programme."[32] In 1778, Howard, with the aid of Sir William Blackstone and Sir William Eden, drafted a Bill providing for a penitentiary, which was passed by the English Parliament in 1779. "The term penitentiary," said Howard, "clearly shows that Parliament had chiefly in view the reformation and amendment of those to be committed to such places of confinement." The purpose of this institution, as stated in the Act, was "by sobriety, cleanliness, and medical assistance, by a regular series of labour, by solitary confinement during the intervals of work, and by due religious instruction to preserve and amend the health of the unhappy offenders, to inure them to habits of industry, to guard them from pernicious company, to accustom them to serious reflection and to teach them both the principles and practice of every Christian and moral duty."

For various reasons such as the paucity of funds, the war with France and the American colonies, no such penitentiary was then erected in England. However, the idea incorporated in the English law of 1779 undoubtedly infleunced the American prison reformers, particularly the Quakers of Pennsylvania. Before that the system of punishment for crimes that prevailed in the American colonies was exactly similar to what obtained in England during the days of the Stuarts. Felonies and even misdemeanours were punished by flogging, branding and mutilation, the stocks and the pillory. Hanging was the most common method of executing criminals. It was carried on publicly and decreed for nearly eighteen offences in various colonies. As was the case in Europe in the same period, "imprisonment was not looked upon as a means of punishment, but was used rather for the purpose of guaranteeing the presence of the offender at his trial and ultimate punishment."[33]

The Quakers of Pennsylvania, however, had been severely criticizing "the profanities and laxities" of earlier penal systems. In 1682, on the initiative of William Penn, the Pennsylvania Assembly passed the Quaker Code which retained the death penalty for homicide only and introduced hard labour in a house of correction as the chief form of punishment for crimes. With the death of Penn in 1718, the old barbarous punishments were revived.

But the success of the Revolution against England gave the colonists a new perspective of life, and they announced to the world that the Americans "hold these truths to be self-evident, that all men are created equal ; that they are endowed by their creator with certain unalienable Rights ; that among these are Life, Liberty, and the pursuit of Happiness."

The translation of "these truths" into statutes and practices, however, turned out to be "a slow and tortuous process."[34] Even Thomas Jefferson, the great champion of liberty and the most "englightened" opponent to Calvinism and Catholicism was not free from the evil influence of the old theories of punishment. In 1797, in "A Bill for Proportioning Crimes and Punishments," Jefferson proposed punishments which must be regarded now as barbarous.

The Bill provided that "whoever shall be guilty of rape, polygamy, or sodomy with man or woman, shall be punished, if a man by castration, if a woman, by cutting through the cartilage of her nose a hole of one half inch in diameter at the least." Further, "Whosoever, on purpose, and of malice forethought, shall maim another, or shall disfigure him, by cutting out or disabling the tongue, slitting or cutting of a nose, lip or ear, branding or otherwise, shall be maimed, or disfigured in like sort : or if that cannot be, for want of the same part, then as nearly as may be, in some other part of at least equal value and estimation, in the opinion of the jury, and moreover shall forfeit one half of his lands and goods to the sufferer."[35]

But the law for prison reform passed in 1777 by the English Parliament on the inspiration of John Howard and Blackstone, exercised a tremendous influence on the American revolutionaries. Pennsylvania again took the lead. In accordance with the directives of the new Constitution of the State, a law was passed in 1786 which replaced execution and corporal punishment with imprisonment and hard labour on public roads. But, instead of removing idleness from among the prisoners, this new form of punishment produced drunkenness, profanity, and indecency on the street, "a public exhibition of the human animal in disgrace."[36]

This so-called reform was, therefore, opposed by Dr. Benjamin Rush[37] and his group consisting of many Quakers and other humanitarians. In 1794, Pennsylvania passed an Act abolishing capital punishment for most crimes and ordered imprisonment without corporal punishment for other offenses. Other American States have since then followed the example of Pennsylvania, subject to such changes as are required by their local conditions.

But two major developments in American penal management have arisen from the acceptance of this new policy, viz., the erection of state prisons as contrasted with county or local prisons and a keen awareness by the people of the need for reformation of the character of criminals. As dangerous criminals ceased to be sentenced to death, the American states had to erect stronger prisons for detaining them for security purposes.[38] But the Quakers of Pennsylvania wrongly thought that the best way to reform criminals was to keep them confined in solitary cells where they would reflect on their crimes, repent and thus be reformed.

This mistake was realised in 1790, when a new Act passed by the legislature of Pennsylvania led to the establishment of Philadelphia's Walnut Street Jail on a revolutionary model. For the first time in the correctional history of America, a crude attempt was made in this little prison to classify inmates so that women, vagrants, debtors, witnesses, misdemeanants and felons would not be intermingled and the disastrous association of criminals could be prevented. The sentenced inmates were sought to be reformed in two ways. The less hardened offenders were put into rather hard labour for which they received wages. They laboured in association at productive trades such as carpentry, weaving, shoe-making, tailoring etc. Except for female prisoners, silence was enforced in the workshops and at meals. The convicted felons were kept in solitary confinment without labour and for this purpose, a separate block of tiny cells was built within the prison yard which became the first penitentiary in America. Religious instruction and weekly services were offered to the prisoners for their reformation. Control of the prison was vasted in "an appointed unpaid board of inspectors" with the novel idea that in prison management voluntary services by citizens would be "humane and efficient." The prison ceased to be "a scene of debauchery, idleness and profanity," and appeared to be a "school of reformation and a place of public labour."[39]

Further improvements in the Penitentiary model were made at Philadelphia in 1829, where a new policy of prison discipline was initiated. The inmates, upon entering the prison, were shut off completely from the outside world until the end of their terms of imprisonment. They were to live and work in separate cells and the architecture of the prison was such that each cell was itself a complete prison up to his occupant. At no time a prisoner was allowed to leave his cell except for doing exercise in a small yard attached to his own cell. The occupations of the inmates were restricted to such handicrafts as spinning, weaving and shoe-making that could be done inside the cell. Sole visitors to the prisoner were the prison officers, moral instructors and official visitors. The only constant companion of the prisoner was the Bible.

But at Auburn in New York, the Quakers developed in 1824 another system where the prisoners worked in congregate shops during the day but lived in separate cells at night. This was intended to assure maximum industrial production as well as to prevent contamination and plotting. "Repressive rules, undeviating routine and cruel punishments, especially flogging, were applied to maintain tight control, the latter an aspect of of life that was not so characteristic of the Pennsylvania system."[40]

There was a long controversy as to the relative merits of the Pennsylvania and the Auburn systems. The Auburn system was initiated in most American states while the Pennsylvania system triumphed in Europe. Both, however, suffered considerable changes in the decades to come.

In *England* the first national *penitentiary* for penal servitude, *Millbank*, was opened *in 1821*. Since then, prisons on a cellular pattern have begun to spread throughout Europe. Two such prisons, for example, were established in *Belgium in 1835* and one in *Germany in 1839*. Following the abandonment of transportation under the Penal Servitude Act of 1857, several national prisons were established in England which, however, were greatly influenced by new prison systems developed in the United States.[41]

Enlightened and humane prison administrators of Europe soon realized that criminals could hardly be reformed through repressive measures retained in the penitentiaries and that their treatment should be so designed as to fit them for return to civil life purged of criminal tendencies. The first experiment on this line was started about 1840 by Captain Alexander Maconochie (1787—1860) at Norfolk Island, an English penal colony of disrepute, located about a thousand miles off the coast of Australia. Immediately after assuming the charge of this penal settlement, Maconochie abolished the old '*flat-time sentence*' and introduced what became known as the *Mark system.* Under this system, each prisoner was debited with a certain number of marks or credits proportional to the gravity of his crime. These he had to earn through work, study and good conduct. The more rapidly he earned the required number of marks, the speedier was his release. In order to restore dignity to the prisoners, degrading punishments were restricted only to cases involving security of the colony. Discipline was maintained by fines expressed in marks and by withdrawal or curtailment of privileges.

This "ingenious" system of Maconochie thus "symbolized the decline of the 'let the punishment fit the crime' theory of correction and presaged the use of indeterminate sentences, individualized treatment and parole. Above all, it emphasized training and performance, rather than solitude, as the chief mechanisms of reformation".[42] Yet, as Barnes and Teeters have rightly observed, Maconochie's enlightenment was nothing but "a momentary gleam in the long night of savagery and benighted bureaucracy that characterized the Australian transportation system. Not only was his progressive correctional philosophy not encouraged, but it was actually undermined and repudiated by his superiors".[43] In 1844, he was relieved of his command of the penal colony at Norfolk Island. But his ideas and experiments paved the way for further advancement of the prison system in Europe as well as in America.

Sir Walter Crofton, as Chairman of the Board of Directors of the Irish prisons, also found that repressive measures had failed to reform the hardened criminals in his charge. He, therefore, resolved to treat them as human beings, not as conveicts and to train them *naturally* to a state of reformation so that they would become easily acceptable to society after release. For the fulfilment of this objective, he introduced what became popularly known as the *Irish system.*

The prisoners under this system progressed through three stages of confinement before their return to civil life. At the *first stage*, a prisoner was confined for at least eight months in a cellular prison at Mountjoy, Dublin, under strict discipline. Then, at the *second stage*, if his conduct was satisfactory, he was transferred to Spike Island Prison to labour on fortifications in association with other inmates. Here, he progressed through four conduct classes. For promotion to the higher conduct class, he had to earn the required number of marks through good conduct, educational performance, and industriousness at work. At the *third stage*, the prisoner was transferred to one of the small intermediate prison units for six months or more before release where he had to work at various projects with sufficient freedom and responsiblity. As Johnson says, "These units served as filters between imprisonment and conditional release. The purpose was to *demonstrate* that the prisoner was being trusted and to show the public that the prisoners *could* be trusted".[44]

The Irish system thus combined in the basic ideal for reformation, thc principles that the time to be served by the prisoner was to be determined by his conduct in prison ; that the promotion to release was to be based on graded stages of increasing freedom and responsibility ; that stress was to be given on the importance of picking up industrious habits to achieve self-reliance ; and that a rudimentary parole system to test the degree of correction attained was to be applied.[45]

In England some ardent prison reformers strongly advocated the Irish system but the press and public sternly opposed it because of the spectacular increase of crime in their country in 1862. In America, on the other hand, the Irish system created a great wave. In 1870,[46] at the first Congress[47] of the National Prison Association[48] was formulated a "Declaration of Principles" which stressed "reformation rather than vindictive suffering" as the principal purpose of prison administration. As Richard A McGee, one of America's foremost prison administrators, has rightly pointed out, "the concept of punishment had not been abandoned then any more than it has today, but was subordinated to the view that the programme of the prisoner should be regulated in such a way as to secure his reformation and resocialization."[49] The Congress adopted the principle of indeterminate sentencing, rewards for good behaviour, parole or conditional release and social training in order to reform and resocialize the offenders.

The Elmira (New York) Reformatory opened in 1876 for the treatment of young and first offenders with Zebulon Brockway as Superintendent was the first American institution to embody these principles. Although the institution created much enthusiasm among the prison reformers, particularly the clergy, it failed to bear fruits because of architectural limitations, overcrowding problems, and lack of adequately trained personnel. The embodiment of the rehabilitation idea in adult prisons did not receive much attention until 1930. Since that year, however, vigorous efforts have been made to introduce radical changes in the prisons for both the adult and the young offenders. Excepting the county jails that have "most successfully resisted change and reform", methods conducive to rehabilitation have been introduced more or less in most of the federal and the state prisons. Other remarkable reforms include the diversification of adult correctional institutions to meet the varying needs of individual prisoners and more individualized training and treatment within the institutions.[50]

Thus, in America today,[51] rehabilitation is no longer "a vague, haphazard and loosely defined process", but a notion translated into considerably effective and practical programmes. The American Correctional Association in their 'Manual for Correctional Standards' have clearly indicated the essential principles of a well-rounded correctional or rehabilitation-oriented programme of individualized training and treatment in an institution for adult offenders which include the following: "Scientific classification and programme-planning on the basis of complete case histories, examinations, tests and studies of the individual prisoners ; adequate medical services ; making ful use of psychiatry ; psychological and sociological services, properly related to the problems of education, work assignment, discipline and preparation for parole ; individual and group therapy and counselling . . . under the direction of psychiatrists, psychologists or other trained therapists and counsellors ; casework services, reaching families as well as prisoners ; employment at tasks comparable in variety, type and pace to the work of the world outside, and especially tasks with vocational training value ; academic and vocational education, in accordance with the individual's needs, interests and capabilities ; library services ; . . . directed recreation ; . . . a religious programme ; . . . discipline that aims at the development of self-control and preparation for free life, not merely conformity to institutional rules ; adequate buildings and equipment. . . and above all, adequate and complete personnel, carefully selected, well trained, and serving under such conditions as to promote a high degree of morale and efficiency".[52]

This revolutionary development in penology in America has not gone unnoticed and unhonoured in the European countries. With the beginning of the present century, the European attitude towards criminals had undergone a change so much so that, as Kaufmann says, "the demand not to hate them but to remain mindful of their humanity no longer sounded utopian". This change was due in no small measure to the novels of Charles Dickens, Victor Hugo, Dostoevsky, Tolstoy, and Zola and the dramas of Ibsen.[53]

In England, for example, Sir Evelyn Ruggles-Brise, director of the English prisons, after studying several American reformatories launched his famous system of *Borstal training* for young offenders of the age-group between sixteen and twenty-one in 1908. The Borstal system was comprised of a variety of institutions, each providing a specified degree of custodial supervision and specializing in a certain kind of training and treatment for young offenders including individualized treatment in the period immediately following release. The chief object of this system "is no longer to punish the offender but to develop his capacity to assume full responsibility for his conduct. The use of recreational, employment, and educational facilities in the outside community is an essential feature of the Borstal system".[54] As Goldfarb and Singer, two leading American experts on Correctional Justice, observe, the Borstal system "was destined to have a far greater impact on corrections than the American reformatory movement that partially inspired it".[55]

Our foregoing study clearly reveals that reformation and rehabilitation of offenders are the fundamental purposes of modern prison administration. The fulfilment of these purposes requires attention to (a) classification of prisoners on scientific lines, (b) their accommodation, (c) health, (d) education, (e) discipline and punishment, and (f) their social rehabilitation.

In the following chapters we shall discuss these conditions of reformation and rehabilitation of offenders in relation to the administration of prisons in India with special reference to West Bengal.

NOTES AND REFERENCES

1. Walter C. Reckless, *The Crime Problem,* First Indian Edn., 1971, p. 497.
2. John C. Ball, "The Deterrence Concept in Criminology and law", *The Journal of Criminal Law, Criminology & Police Science*, (North-western University School of Law), Vol. 44, No. 3, 1955.
3. John Lewis Gillin, *Criminology & Penology,* rev. edn., 1935, pp. 203-204 ; See also Reckless, *op. cit.*, p. 497.
4. This statement was quoted in the great *Digest* compiled under the direction of Justinian I in 533—See *Encyclopedia Americana*, 1966, Vol. 22, p. 606.
5. *Encyclopedia Americana, op. cit.*, p. 606.
6. Ronald L. Goldfarb & Linda R. Singer, *After Conviction*, 1973, p. 21.
7. *Encyclopedia Americana, op. cit.*, p. 606.
8. Edwin H. Sutherland and Donald R. Cressey, *Principles of Criminology*, Sixth edn., 2nd Indian Reprint, 1968, p. 270.
9. *Encyclopaedia of the Social Sciences*, Ed., Edwin R.A. Seligman, 15th Printing, 1963, Vol. VII, p. 616.
10. Sutherland & Cressey, *op. cit.*, p. 270.
11. *Encyclopedia Americana. op. cit..* p. 606.
12. Sutherland & Cressey, *op. cit.*, p. 270 & *Encyclopedia Americana, op. cit.*, p. 606.
13. Sutherland & Cressey, *op. cit.*, p. 270.
14. Donald R. Taft & Ralph W. England, Jr., *Criminology*, 4th edn., 1964, p. 394.
15. George Ives, *A History of Penal methods*, 1914, p. 10 ; See also Taft & England, Jr., *op. cit.*, p. 394.
16. Harry Elmer Barnes & Negley K. Teeters, *New Horizons in Criminology*, Indian edn., 1966, p. 389.
17. Taft and England, Jr. *op. cit.*, p. 394.
18. Barnes and Teeters, *op. cit.*, p. 390.
19. Sutherland and Cressey, *op. cit.*, p. 270.

20. Max Grunhut, *Penal Reform : A Comparative Study*, 1948 ; See also Reckless, *op. cit.*, p. 545.
21. *Encyclopaedia of the Social Sciences*, Ed., Seligman, 13th Printing, 1959, Vol. XII, p. 57.
22. *Encyclopedia Americana*, *op. cit.*, p. 606.
23. Reckless, *op. cit.*, p. 545.
24. Reckless, *op. cit.*, p. 546.
25. *Encyclopaedia Britannica*, 1967, Vol. 18, p. 557.
26. Reckless, *op. cit.*, p. 546.
27. Goldfarb & Singer, *op. cit.*, pp. 19-20.
28. Walter Kaufmann, *Without Guilt and Justice*, pp. 43-44.
29. Harry E. Barnes, *Society in Transition*, 1939, p. 724 ; See also Taft and England, Jr., *op. cit.*, p. 395.
30. Reckless, *op. cit.*, p. 546.
31. *Encyclopaedia Britannica*, *op. cit.*, p. 557.
32. Barnes & Teeters, *op. cit.*, p. 334.
33. Richard A. McGee, "What's Past Is Prologue", *The Annals of the American Academy of Political and Social Science*, Vol. 381, January 1969, p. 2.
34. *Ibid.*, p. 3.
35. Kaufmann, *op. cit.*, p. 42.
36. Taft and England, Jr., *op. cit.*, p. 404.
37. An eminent physician and penologist who also signed the Declaration of Independence.
38. Sutherland and Cressey, *op. cit.*, p. 447.
39. Francis C. Gray, *Prison Discipline in America*, 1948, p. 22 ; See also Elmer Hubert Johnson, *Crime, Correction, and Society*, Rev. edn., 1968, pp. 482-83.
40. Goldfarb and Singer, *op, cit.*, pp. 29-30.
41. Taft and England, Jr., *op. cit.*, p. 402.
42. *Encyclopaedia Britannica*, *op. cit.*, p. 557.
43. Barnes & Teeters, *op. cit.*, p. 422.
44. Johnson, *op. cit.*, p. 493.
45. Barnes and Teeters, *op. cit.*, pp. 423-24.
46. According to the American Correctional Association, "The 1870s was a period which, it appeared at time, might mark the beginning of a 'Golden Age of Penology"—See *Manual for Correctional Standards*, 1968, p. 11.
47. Held in Cincinnati.
48. Later known as the American Prison Association, and now known as the American Correctional Association.

49. Mc Gee, *op. cit.*, p. 7.
50. American Correctional Association, New York, *Manual for Correctional Standards*, Third Printing, 1968, p. 17.
51. A public poll (Harris Survey), held in 1966, indicates that 77 per cent of the people in America believe that rehabilitation should be the central purpose of correctional practice—See Mc Gee, *op. cit.*, p. 7.
52. American correctional Association, *op. cit*,, pp. 18-19.
53. Kaufmann, *op. cit.*, pp. 48-49.
54. *Encyclopaedia Britannica*, *op. cit.*, p. 558.
55. Goldfarb and Singer, *op. cit.*, p. 44.

3

CLASSIFICATION OF PRISONERS

The justification of an administration rests primarily on its success in achieving its fundamental objects. The fundamental objects of prison administration, as already discussed, are to wean the offender away from wrong-doing in future and make his return to society safe and useful. To achieve these ends classification of prisoners on scientific lines is of utmost importance for, without such classification individualized treatment through which prisons now seek to attain their basic objects is impossible.

Scientific classification is necessary from the point of view of national interest too. While classifying prisoners we may be able to obtain the basic materials for empirical studies on crime and deviance and know the social background and the individual eccentricity of the criminal. The classification as well as the number of criminals in each class give us an insight into the dynamics of our socio-economic life and are therefore, an invaluable aid to social reform and reconstruction. Classification would also help us understand the interrelation of different categories of crimes. We may notice at the time of classification that an increase or decrease in the number of a particular type of offenders is followed by a corresponding increase or decrease in the number of another type of offenders. An increase of prisoners convicted for sex crimes, for instance, may lead to an increase of persons convicted for drunkenness or forgery. Such a finding will be of immense help to the sociologists, psychologists or the criminologists in understanding the complexity of crimes. This would also help the legislature in making laws more rationally for public order and security. As for the police, it would be possible to move from the detected to undetected areas of criminal activities and hence to provide greater protection to society.

Another great advantage of classification is that it prevents the evil effects of contamination of prisoners having varying degrees of criminality. Classification would also enable the prison administration to provide different types of treatment to different categories of prisoners according to their individual capacities and needs for reform and rehabilitation. Experience of even the early prison reformers reveals that worst psychological troubles are bound to arise if prisoners are huddled together irrespective of their crime peculiarities. Any attempt to eliminate or regulate criminal propensities cannot succeed without the requisite knowledge of the history of a crime and of the family background, mode of living, education, culture and other aspects of life of the criminal. These objective differences serve as the basis for different types of treatment in the matter of food, lodging, work-assignments, recreation, intellectual and reformatory courses, etc., for different categories of prisoners.

The principal objectives of classification as laid down in the All India Jail Manual Committee's *Model Prison Manual*[1] are :

(i) to study the offender as an individual ; to understand sequence of his criminal behaviour and the problems presented by him ;

(ii) to segregate inmates into homogeneous groups for the purpose of treatment ;

(iii) to organize an overall, balanced, integrated and individualized training and treatment programme ;

(iv) to review the inmate's response to institutional regime and treatment and to adjust the programme to suit his needs ;

(v) to coordinate and integrate all institutional activities and to develop a system of constructive institutional discipline ; to maintain a uniform continuity in various phases of institutional management ;

(vi) to ensure maximum utilization of resources and treatment facilities available in the institution as well as the community.

Scientific classification is thus the basis of individualized correctional treatment, which includes proper custody, discipline and work assignment. The *Handbook of Classification*, prepared as far back as 1947 by the American Correctional Association, points out in greater detail the advantages of classification, as follows :

1. Proper segregation of different type of offenders.
2. More adequate custodial supervision and control.
3. Better discipline.
4. Increased productivity of inmates.
5. More effective organization of all training and treatment facilities.
6. Greater continuity in the training and treatment programme.
7. Higher personnel morale.
8. Better inmate attitude.
9. Reduced failures of released prisoners.
10. Better guides in long range planning of building requirements.
11. Classification reports may have many unpredictable values.[2]

It is obvious that classification in prison should be based on certain principles, viz., age, sex, physical and mental condition, educational and vocational training needs and potentialities for reformation and rehabilitation. Besides, factors like nature of crimes, motives, provocations, previous history of the offender, his "social processing", his "sophistication in crime" should be taken into account to determine his gradation in custody and appropriate treatment.

Some modern criminologists, however, are of the opinion that the nature of crimes need not be taken into consideration while classifying prisoners on the plea that the nature of a person's offence is not a measure of his potentiality for rehabilitation. As Barnes and Teeters say, for instance, "The function of classification is to differentiate the various inmates . . . in terms of their potentialities for rehabilitation regardless of the offence on the sentence".[3] It cannot be denied that the nature of a person's offence is not a measure of his potentiality for rehabilitation. Even so, in order to avoid the evil effects of an over-optimistic assessment of the criminal and also of uncontrolled mixing and consequent contamination, the nature of crimes should reasonably be taken into account for the purpose of classification of offenders in prison. If a prisoner convicted for an organized crime such as wagon-breaking or smuggling is kept with the petty or first offenders on the unproved ground that their chances of rehabilitation are more or less equal, the possibility of contamination and worsening of community life would remain very great. While classifying prisoners the nature of crimes should, therefore, receive due attention.

Scientific classification of prisoners has been accepted as an essential element of modern prison system and there is no reason why it should not be adopted in the administration of jails in India. It is often argued that scientific classification involves huge expenditure as it requires a large number of professional personnel in prison administration. American experience, however, does not confirm this view altogether. According to American Correctional Association's Handbook,[4] "a classification programme is not entirely dependent upon a full staff of professional personnel, well-trained management people, and extensive treatment facilities, although the programme can be more effective to the extent that these conditions exist. The correctional system with little by way of professional staff or facilities, if it still attempts to apply the principles of classification, may achieve thereby a more effective use of its resources in individualized treatment."

In India classification was practically unknown until the greater part of the last century. The Report of the Prison Discipline Committee of 1836-38 observed, "In the Bombay House of Correction women, thieves, young offenders and old offenders are kept in separate place by night, but not by day. In the Calcutta House of Correction the Classification is still more defective . . . Old and young offenders are here mixed up indiscriminately by day or by night. In the other goals . . . there is no classification or separation whatever, either of males or females, by day or by night".[5] The report of Mary Carpenter, an eminent social worker who visited some Indian jails later, also contained almost identical observation. The report, published in 1867, records "Criminals of all classes, old and young, male and female, are in our ordinary Indian prisons mixed and mingled together like *brute beasts* than human beings,—one cell in many cases common to all, one treatment the lot of all, . . . no classification of prisons,. . . the most serious contamination could not be avoided . . and any boys who entered the jail were irrevocably plunged into a life of crime . . . the wretched prisoners, after ten hours of labour, are locked up in the dark for twelve hours in the worst possible association."[6]

Classification of prisoners, at least in some measure, was attempted to have introduced in Indian prisons when the government orders regarding habitual offenders were issued in 1886. However, the report of the Bombay Jail Reforms Committee of 1948 observed that till then in actual practice this separation of habituals even was very imperfectly carried out and that "except for the separation of the females from the male prisoners nowhere separation was really complete".[7]

As the concepts of correctional treatment became popular in the early present century, the need for segregation of offenders on the basis of essential principles of scientific classification was emphasized by the Indian Jails Committee of 1919-20 as well as the Jail Reforms Committees of several States. However, as late as 1959, the report of the All-India Jail Manual Committee observed that "owing to factors like overcrowding, inadequate buildings, influx of prisoners sentenced to short terms of imprisonment, inadequate segregation facilities, insufficient staff and supervisory organization, the conventional and deeply rooted idea of running prisons in as *cheap* a manner as possible", the principle of segregation of prisoners of various categories could not have been fully implemented.[8]

The existing jail codes of various States and Union Territories provide for segregation of prisoners more or less on the basis of their age, sex, criminal antecedents, nature and terms of imprisonment, physical and mental conditions, etc. These minimum statutory requirements, though not enough for the purpose of scientific classification, are more in breach than in observance. As the latest All India Committee on Jail Reforms (1980-83), during its visits to various States and Union Territories, observed, "undertrial prisoners, prisoners sentenced to short, medium and long terms of imprisonment, prisoners sentenced to simple imprisonment, habitual offenders, lifers, hardened and dangerous prisoners, children, young offenders, women offenders, civil prisoners, prisoners sentenced by court martial, criminal and non-criminal lunatics, detenus under the National Security Act, persons detained under the Conservation of Foreign Exchange and Prevention of Smuggling Activities Act, smugglers, etc., were all kept in the same institutions and the arrangemen s for their segregation even in different wards were not effective". The committee further observed that "factors like overcrowding and periodic large turnover of prisoners override all principles and requirements of segregation" and, that "in reality segregation has become a provision only on paper".[9]

Under Rule 616 of the West Bengal Jail Code[10], in every jail each of the following classes of prisoners is to be kept entirely separate from others :

1. Civil prisoners.
2. Undertrial prisoners.
3. Female prisoners.
4. Male prisoners under twenty-one years of age.
5. Male prisoners who have not arrived at the age of puberty.
6. Other male convicted prisoners.

Rule 617 provides for classification of convicted prisoners into three Divisions, viz., Division I, Division II and Division III, on the basis of character, social status, education, habit of life and nature of offences. Rule 617B provides for classification of undertrial prisoners into two Divisions, viz. Division I undertrial and Division II undertrial, on the basis of social status, education and habit of life. Besides, the code also prescribes separation, as much as possible, of casual prisoners from habitual ones, separation of prisoners sentenced to simple imprisonment from those sentenced to rigorous imprisonment, and segregation of leper prisoners as well as prisoners suffering from tuberculosis, venereal and grave infectious diseases from other prisoners.[11]

Classification of prisoners into Divisions I, II, III or I and II according to social status, education and mode of living is a matter of controversy. Some penologists in Uttar Pradesh hold that "education and good position should be regarded as an aggravating circumstance in regard to crime rather than an excuse . . . to those who in spite of the advantages of station and education fall into crime". Reviewing this problem a conscientious critic observes, "It may be argued that the very fact of incarceration is sufficient and there is no need to impose needless physical sufferings on a person by according him a treatment which substantially differs from what he is accustomed to outside, and that there should be some relationship between the prisoner's life in prison and his life outside. According to this view, life in a prison needs not be a luxury but it should approximate to the life outside ; and if it is intended to reform him, his normal necessities should be provided. It is certainly *convenient* to classify prisoners according to their social status, requirements of food, etc., but really speaking it is *neither reasonable nor proper*".[12] The All India Jail Manual Committee of 1957-59 also made the pertinent observation : "We hope that eventually there would be no such division. However, so long as different classes and different modes of living prevail in society, we consider that with a view to avoiding undue hardship and misery, it would be desirable to classify prisoners into two Divisions, viz., Division A and Division B. As the social stratification gets merged and as the fusion of the social classes becomes more extensive, this division may be gradually done away with."[13] But, we think it necessary that until such classification is totally abolished, there should be severe restrictions in awarding the higher Division so that the ordinary convicts, particularly the *white-collar* criminals such as adulterators, black-marketeers, forgers, smugglers, defalcators could not take any undue advantage of their social status in obtaining the higher division.

There are varieties of crimes such as sedition, murder, theft, riot, sex offence, adulteration, hoarding, black-marketing, forgery, etc. As each crime differs from others in respect of nature and gravity, our ancient law-givers prescribed different punishments for different crimes. In our present Penal Code too different punishments have been provided for different types of offence. Variation of crimes and consequential variation in punishments require scientific classification of prisoners. Moreover, as the report of the All India Jail Manual Committee of 1957-59 observes, "The pattern of delinquency and crime in India is definitely changing. The techniques of organized and professional criminality are already showing some marked and significant changes. It is, therefore, necessary to deal with these problems on a scientific basis. Such a scientific approach will become possible only through scientific classification of prisoners".[14]

The purpose of scientific classification is not fulfilled by mere segregation of offenders on the basis of certain principles. In fact, for the scientific handling of prisoners, classification is the first step in "a continuous process of individualizing correctional treatment" till release of the prisoners. A well-planned and coordinated system of classification and reclassification makes the correctional course dynamic.

In our *Model Prison Manual*,[15] classification and reclassification work have been directed to be phased as under the following stages :

1. Admission—quarantine—orientation ;
2. Study of the offender through (a) interview, (b) collec-

tion of social information, (c) tests and examinations, (d) observation ;

3. Analysis of the collected material, compilation of various reports, preparation of the case file, central indexing ;
4. Planning of training and treatment, implementation of the same and observation of response to treatment programmes ;
5. Review of progress and reclassification, adjusting institutional programme to the needs of the inmates ;
6. Planning post-release rehabilitation programme in collaboration with the aftercare service ;
7. Pre-release preparation ;
8. Release procedure.

Thus, classification, a continuous process begins, upon the reception of the inmate. The *Manual*[16] lays down the following procedure which should generally be adopted at the time of initial classification of inmates :

1. As far as practicable, advance rotation of the case file amongst the members of the classification committee ;
2. A brief oral summary of each case by the Deputy Superintendent in charge of classification ; discussion of the case ; understanding the sequence of the inmate's criminal behaviour and the problems presented by him ;
3. Chalking out the institutional training and treatment programme for the inmates on the basis of their individual needs while taking decisions on (a) transfer if found necessary, (b) gradation in custody, (c) medical matters, (d) individual problems of the inmate, (e) work, employment, vocational training, (f) education, (g) social adjustment, (h) special instructions, if any, to personnel about collection of more information, special precautions to be taken if any etc., and (i) date of reclassification ;
4. Informing the inmate about the programme chalked

out for him, modifying the programme if found necessary ;

5. Recording of decisions taken and communicating the same to the concerned staff members.

After initial classification as per the above procedure is over, the prisoners are to be removed from the quarantine area and sent to various sections of the institution.

Chalking out the institutional training and treatment programme for the inmates is not enough. The ultimate success of a classification system rests on the inmates' response to such programme. The *Manual*, therefore, provides for observation of the inmates' response to institutional programme as well as review of their progress or reclassification. It lays down under Rule 8 that the officers-in-charge of various sections and programmes will maintain progress reports containing information about the inmate's adjustment to institutional life, his discipline, the interest taken by him in various programmes, any marked change in his habits, attitudes and behaviour, etc. The reports should be written at least once in a quarter or more often if necessary and sent at the end of each quarter to the Deputy Superintendent in charge of classification work.

Again, under Rule 9 (i) of the *Manual* the review of progress or reclassification work is to be done by the Classification Committee. The work should continue from the inmates' initial classification till their release and the functions of the committee in this respect would be :

(a) to study the inmates' response to institutional training and treatment ;

(b) to make necessary modifications and changes in training and treatment programme ;

(c) to make recommendations about transfer to other institution having a different line of training and treatment ;

(d) to examine whether the inmate has reached peak points of institutional impacts and whether he is getting stagnated in a particular institutional activity ;

(e) to determine whether the inmate is fit for being transferred to a semi-open or open institution ;
(f) to formulate plans for post-release rehabilitation programmes in collaboration with the after-care-service ;
(g) to provide instructions for pre-release preparation and release planning.

Rule 9 (iii) requires that "When cases of inmates are being reviewed by the Classification Committee the Assistant Superintendents, technical and educational personnel and senior members of the guarding staff from the respective areas should as far as is practicable attend the meetings of the Committee." It is expected that such association of the field staff would enable the Committee to review the cases on the basis of first hand information and to change and adjust the treatment programme on practical and realistic lines.

The laudable objectives of this continuous and progressive scientific classification can not be attained unless the scheme is ideal, that is, perfect in other respects as well. To make it such it is necessary that there should be a cer alized authority in each state to control all matters relatir to classification work. Such control will facilitate integration and coordination of classification work in all the institutions. In America, for instance, with a strong centralized authority as found now in many states, each institution becomes an integral unit in the whole system and a specific functional unit in the placement of offenders.[17] The All India Jail Manual Committee of 1957-59 thus aptly recommended the setting up of the Classification Branch in the State Head Quarters Office to be staffed by personnel having the requisite training, experience and insight in this field.[18]

It is also necessary that there should be separate establishments for each well-pronounced group, i.e., diversification of institutions, so that the inmates can be grouped for a homogeneous system of reformative training and treatment appropriate to their individual needs. "Diversification of institutions," as the report of this Committee observes, "can be achieved through basic segregation, gradation in security measures, treatment emphasis and institutional programme content".[19] A net-work of diversified institutions on this basis has been stipulated by the Committee in its *Model Prison Manual.* The broad categories of such institutions included in the *Manual* are :

(i) Institutions for delinquent children ;
(ii) Institutions for adolescent offenders ;
(iii) Institutions for non-habitual adult offenders ;
(iv) Institutions for habitual, professional and organized criminals ;
(v) Special Institution for difficult discipline cases ;
(vi) Annexes or institutions for women offenders ;
(vii) Units for inmates suffering from mental disorders ;
(viii) Units for old and infirm inmates ;
(ix) Leprosy units ;
(x) T.B. units ;
(xi) Annexes or institutions for undertrial prisoners ;
(xii) Sub jails ;
(xiii) Open institutions.[20]

Again, diversification of institutions would be meaningless unless there is an arrangement for transfer of prisoners from one type of institutions to another when and where necessary. An ideal classification scheme, therefore, requires systematic arrangement for such transfer. However, while handling the case of transfer, precautions should be taken so that the inmate is not deprived of his family contacts as a result of transfer.

Another important point is that the Classification Committee which decides upon an inmate's programme or assignment including changes and modifications should be a multi- disciplinary body consisting of experts like psychologists, psychiatrists, criminologists, sociologists as well as prison medical and welfare officers and trained custodial personnel. It is necessary that the experts are recruited from outside. "A psychologist who by intelligence test will provide factual information about the delinquent, a psychiatrist who will have to suggest a cure of psychosis or psychopathic conditions, for example, will generally fail to gain the confidence of the prisoners if he is looked upon as a part of the custodial institution. So much depends upon their willing response. That is why these specialists should come from outside. They should not sink into dull lethargic formality or forget the goal of individulization based on personal contact".[21] The inclusion of trained custodial personnel in the Committee is also necessary for giving desired assistance to the inmates. "Real classification", as Barnes and Teeters have aptly explained, "means the best possible help that can be extended to the inmate. A group of specialists is important ; so is a trained custodial force, a staff of men and women who have some notion of what the programme means, who are in sympathy with it, and will manifest a degree of . . . sympathetic insight".[22]

If the provisions laid down in *Model Prison Manual*[23] are to be followed, there should be in each Central and District Prison and also in such other institution as may be specified by the Inspector General a Classification Committee consisting of the following personnel :

(a) Chairman —Superintendent.
(b) Vice-Chairman —Deputy Superintendent.
(c) Members —Deputy Superintendent-in-charge-of Production and Vocational Training, Medical Officer, Correctional Social Worker and Education Officer.
(d) Member Secretary—Officer-in-charge of the Reception Unit.

In addition, experts like psychologists, psychiatrists and criminologists would be associated, wherever possible, with the work of the Committee. The composition of the Committee would vary according to the type of the institution and the institution staff organization.

In its Chapter X the *Manual* has been careful to lay down certain guiding principles regarding recruitment and training of correctional personnel including guarding staff.

It has been properly decided that an ideal classification scheme requires actual participation of the inmate in the planning of programme or assignment for himself. The experience of prison administrators in advanced countries of the West clearly reveals that in the absence of such participation, the treatment programme becomes meaningless, superficial and superimposed. Hence, Barnes and Teeters suggest that as far as it is reasonably practical, "the inmate must share in the planning, must assume responsibility for it. The staff of the (classification) clinic can help him, but the real decision must rest with him".[24]

Since the classification of inmates on scientific lines is rational with laudable objects behind it, our prison administration should introduce it as far as possible under given circumstances. The All India Jail Manual Committee of 1957-59, while laying down the guiding principles regarding mechanism and method of classification, have found that the introduction of scientific classification would not initially involves much expenditure. "With proper organizational methods in correctional administration, proper definition of responsibilities and authorities and proper decentralization of functions, it should be possible to deploy some members of the executive staff having requisite training and abilities for the initial organization of classification work".[25] What is thus required is a well-planned scheme of scientific classification. To start with, the work may be undertaken at least in one institution of each state so that on the basis of the experience gained in such pilot project, the work could be extended to other institutions gradually.[26] Meanwhile, the inmates of other institutions which await the beginning should at least be housed in such a manner that the positive evils of contamination are avoided.

As in other States the existing system of classification of prisoners in West Bengal is "old and archaic" and not based on any scientific principles. In the Alipore Central Jail, however, apart from the normal classification as per the rules of the Jail Code, the casual convicts are classified into two groups—the physically and/or mentally disabled and the normally healthy—on the basis of the recommendations of the Welfare Officer, the Psychologist and the Medical Officer. Classification even in this institution is far from the goal of scientific classification.

As regards the diversification of correctional institutions which is the essence of scientific classification, the picture is equally gloomy. To quote the report of the West Bengal Jail Code Revision Committee of 1972-73, "There are at present prisons for adult, but none exclusively for any particular type of prisoners. There are no jails meant exclusively for women or for juveniles ; for long-term or short-term prisoners ; for hardened incorrigibles ; for casual or undertrial prisoners. Nor have we any 'open prisons' as in eleven other States of India".[27]

It is encouraging to note that the present Left Front Government have of late taken certain positive steps in this matter. More than hundred destitute and neglected boys have already been removed from ordinary prisons to the Institute of Correctional Services in Barasat which was set up in 1974 by the then Congress (I) Government for Naxalite prisoners of a certain age group. While some of these boys now study in schools outside, others are studying in a school in the Institute. General education apart, the school offers eight type of vocational training. The Institute provides facilities for physical training and games and has a television set and a radio. The first prison for women has also been opened in Burdwan in 1984. Such efforts, insufficient howsoever they are, may be considered as a welcome move towards the beginning of the process of diversification of prisons and correctional institutions.

The West Bengal Jail Code Revision Committee of 1972-73 reasonably held that the present practice of classifying prisoners into merely civil prisoners, undertrial prisoners, female prisoners, etc., should be completely abandoned and immediately substituted by a classification process based on the analysis of every prisoner's case history and the psychological and psychiatric investigation of prisoners conducted by professionally trained personnel at the time of their admission. The following are some of the guidelines laid down by this Committee[28] regarding classification of prisoners on modern scientific lines :

1. (a) The Classification Committee for the purpose of scientific grouping and treatment of prisoners must

be set up without delay to ensure the operation of the correctional programme in the diversified institutions on scientific lines.

(b) The Committee composed mainly of psychologists, psychiatrists, sociologists, prison medical officers and prison executives shall decide upon a programme of individualized treatment and training based upon the diagnosis of the offender. It shall then assign him to a designated type of custody, a certain kind of cell or dormitory, a job deemed suitable for him, an educational class suited to his needs, recreations in which he will find interest, and to other activities and services calculated to unfold and develop his healthy potentialities.

(c) The Committee shall have the responsibility of seeing that its recommendations are being actually carried out. There must not be any *forgotten men* in the prisons.

2. Adequate safeguards need to be taken against the pitfalls experienced by prison administrators in actual practice even in the advanced countries of the West. They have found that even if the diagnostic findings are accurate, the treatment planned for the inmates might not be based on them. In some institutions the Classification Committee never meets or meets only rarely and the decisions regarding programme planning are taken by one person only, usually a prison executive. In other institutions the Classification Committee meets regularly, but bases its decision not on the individual needs for a specific kind of treatment of a prisoner but on the custodial and punitive considerations of a cotrectional institution. For example, an inmate who needs vocational training may be assigned to kitchen duties because some one has to do the maintenance work. Sometimes the professional staff may be extremely negligen in carrying out its own recommendations. They keep themselves so busy in writing reports and attendin meetings that they find little time to perform

their duties as administrators of the recommended programmes. Thus, very often, the treatment programme become meaningless and superficial. It is, therefore, necessary that one should be on guard against these eventualities from the very beginning. Opportunism or convenience of the custodial staff should never be allowed to take precedence over institutional treatment aimed at reclamation of offenders.

3. There should be constant evaluation of prisoners to reclassify them according to the varying correctional needs of each.

4. The classification as well as the reclassification procedure should continue from the time of first admission to that of final release from custody.

5. The Reception Centre or the Guidance Centre which is the most recent innovation in the field of classification, should be set up in prisons. The difference between classification of prisoners based on the advice of the Guidance Centres and that based merely on custody-convenience is enormous. As custodial classification, in terms of security risk, is unrelated to the programme of correction, classification which to-day has become synonymous with individualized treatment requires extensive compromise with the all-important "custody". Consequently, treatment programme for the correction of offenders must be cautiously attempted and within the framework of custody.

6. (a) The correctional institutions must be diversified on the basis of the homogeneous grouping of prisoners (as recommended by the Classification Committee), due consideration being given to the security aspects of the different kinds of prisons.

   (b) There must be maximum-security prisons (or cells) for the hard-core, incorrigible and dangerous prisoners, and minimum-security prisons for properly screened better types ; there should also be open agricultural prisons for cultivators who present little security risk ; prisons for dangerous "politicals"; completely separate prisons for undertrials, and so on.

(c) To start with and to save cost the existing prisons may be so remodelled that each prison may serve the purpose of several prisons in one boundary. This diversification will have to be based on the principle of scientific classification of prisoners on admission. Each group of classified prisoners will be placed under a correctional unit earmarked for it. But before an individual prisoner goes to occupy his place in the proper unit, he has to be won over to the idea that the prison staff is there to help him and that he should help himself and compensate for the loss of the precious days of his life by cooperating with the correctional programme intended for him. This is to be done when a prisoner in a reception centre is being studied during his quarantine from the social, medical, psychological, vocational and educational angles to find out what kind of prison programme will suit him best.

7. The principle of transferring a prisoner from one institution to another should be accepted in his interest if the Classfication Committee so recommends. A progressive prisoner should be transferred from maximum security to minimum security, from restricted activities to activities involving greater responsibility and from one kind of training to another kind of training. On the other hand, a regressive or obdurate prisoner, lazy and disobedient, has to be sent to institutions meant for obtuse or recalcitrant chaps.

Conclusion

Scientific classification of prisoners is the essence of modern reformative treatment of offenders. We have discussed in this chapter various guiding principles and methods of scientific classification of prisoners recommended by the All India Jail Manual Committee of 1957-59 in its 'Model Prison Manual' and the West Bengal Jail Code Revision Committee of 1972-73 in its report to the State Government. These recommendations deserve serious attention of the Central and State Governments and need to be adopted and implemented if we really want our prisons to be reformatories. This undoubtedly means a *revolution* in the whole system, involving more expense and requiring a different type of men to operate the new system. "But additional expense," as the Father of our Nation, Mahatma Gandhi, said long ago,[29] "will mean economy in the long run. The greatest advantage of the proposed revolution would no doubt be a reduction in the crimes and reformation of prisoners. The Jails would then be reformatories representing to society sinners as its reformed and respectable members. This may be a far-off event. If we were not under the spell of a longlived custom we should not find it difficult task to turn our prisons into reformatories."

NOTES AND REFERENCES

1. Government of India, 1960, p. 104.
2. American Correctional Association, *Handbook on Classification in Correctional Institutions*, 1947, p. 2.
3. Harry Elmer Barnes and Negley K. Teeters, *New Horizons in Criminology*, Indian edn., 1966, p. 467.
4. *Op. cit.*, pp. 353-54.
5. Para 40 of the Committee's Report.
6. See B.K. Bhattacharya, *Prisons*, 1958, Appendix II, p. 135.
7. *Ibid.*, p. 20.
8. Report of the Committee, Para 29.
9. Report of the Committee, Vol. I, p. 108.
10. Government of West Bengal, Eighth edn., 1967, Vol. I, Part I.
11. See Rules 626, 934, 1046-49, 1242 and 1265 of the West Bengal Jail Code.
12. B.K. Bhattacharya, *op. cit.*, p. 26.
13. Para 65 of the Committee's Report.
14. Para 178 of the Committee's Report.
15. Chap XIX, Rule 4.
16. Vide Chap. XIX, Rules 6 and 7.
17. Barnes and Teeters, *op. cit.*, p. 468.
18. Para 178 (vi) of the Committee's Report.
19. Para 34 (i) of the Committee's Report.

20. Government of India, *Model Prison Manual,* 1960, Chap. III, Rule 1.
21. B.K. Bhattacharya, *op. cit.*, p. 17.
22. Barnes and Teeters, *op. cit.*, p. 476.
23. Chap. XIX, Rule 2.
24. Barnes and Teeters, *op, cit.*, p. 476.
25. Para 179 of the Committee's Report.
26. Vide Para 178(v) of the Committee's Report.
27. Report of the Committee, p. 26.
28. *Ibid.*, pp. 24-26, 52, 62-63 and 66.
29. "My Jail Experience", *Young India*, May 8, 1924.

4

ACCOMMODATION IN PRISONS

Accommodation generally implies lodging and housing. In the context of jail-life, however, it me: as a place where the prisoner can be confined safely to serve his sentence under such living conditions as conducive to correctional treatment and maintenance of basic minimum standards of human dignity. Unlike the ancient or the medieval periods, accommodation in prison nowadays is expected to be fair accommodation. The term 'fair' is a very common concept applied to the entire gamut of modern life. We often speak of fair business, fair politics, fair trial and so forth. Having the imperatives of modern civilization in mind we should better start with a concept of fair accommodation for a prisoner which, in any kind of prison-setting, implies the accommodation required by an inmate for different purposes such as sleeping, bathing, dining, work, study, recreation, physical exercise, etc. However, the total accommodation for the prisoners in a jail or correctional institution has to be little more than the fair accommodation required by all the inmates. For, space is also necessary for the office staff and the menials.

Utilities of Separate Accommodation for the Prisoners

The necessity of providing separate accommodation for

different categories of prisoners was appreciated time and again by a number of official committees and commissions during the colonial rule in India. The prison administrators and policy makers even in those days realized that insufficient accommodation and indiscriminate huddling of prisoners were detrimental not only to the maintenance of discipline and peace in prisons but also to the accomplishment of the correctional objectives of imprisonment. However, the colonial policy of "running prisons in as cheap a manner as possible" stood as an obstacle to any appreciable improvement in the living conditions in prisons. In the present era of individualized training and treatment of offenders separate accommodation for each category of prisoners is considered to be an essential element of correction-oriented prison system for, without separate accommodation scientific classification which is the basis of individualized training and treatment becomes an impossibility.

Separate accommodation is necessary for resocialization of the offenders too. Criminological studies have revealed that a man commits crime in a moment of mental aberration when his good senses are feeble and criminal impulses dominant. After the commission of the crime he may begin to repent and regain his moral self. As Dr. Radhakrishnan has said, "There are no individuals who are utterly evil. . . The spirit is in every one, as a part of oneself, a part of the substratum of one's being. It may be buried in some like a hidden treasure, beneath a barren debris of brutality and violence but it is there all the same, operative and alive, ready to come to the surface at the first suitable opportunity". Therefore, resocialization is possible for a fallen man, if the environment is made favourable for this change. Nothing is more important for this than a suitable accommodation. To impart education to a child, it is essential that his mind should be diverted from games and other amusements and concentrated on studies. Similarly, to reform a prisoner, it is necessary that his mind should be set on healthy ideas and not criminal thinking. Again, for his detachment from evil association and thinking he must require privacy, atleast in some considerable measure. The process of regeneration cannot begin in a crowded atmosphere in which sobriety is held in suspense and blind emotions and passions rule the mind.

Problem of Overcrowding in Prisons

Overcrowding in prisons poses a very difficult and delicate problem to most of the governments today. Even in developed countries like America and England the reformative purpose of prison system is being distorted considerably due to this problem. On 30 June, 1983 federal and state correctional facilities in the United States were incarcerating 4, 31, 829 men and women, an increase of 4.2 per cent over the previous year.[1] The rapid growth of sentenced state and federal prisoners in this country in recent years is graphed in Figure 1. According to a current estimate, the correctional authority incarcerate about one out of every 600 Americans.[2]

Figure 1

Number of sentenced State and Federal Prisoners in the U.S.A Yearend 1925—Midyear 1983

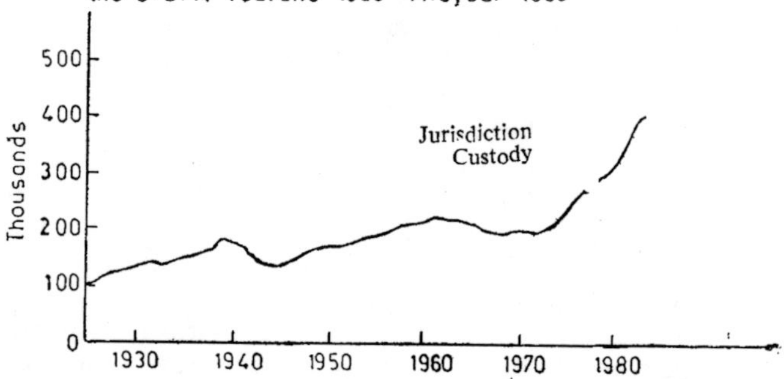

Source : *U.S. Department of Justice,* Prisoners at Midyear 1983 (*Washington, D.C., Government Printing Office, October 1983*), *p. 1* ; Reproduced in Sue Titus Reid, *Crime and Criminology,* Fourth edn., 1985, p. 519.

The situation with regard to jails which house both offenders awaiting trial and those serving short sentences, is even more distressing. Since there is no centralized administration of American jails—whether national or regional, there is no way to proportionately distribute their population. As Goldfarb and Singer pointed out, "Most big-city jails and some county jails are chronically overcrowded, with as many as four inmates housed in six-by-nine-foot cells, sleeping on the floor and confined to their cells on a narrow adjoining corridor for meals and "recreation". Others, generally in rural areas, are often half-empty. Since some jails have from only one to ten sentenced prisoners in custody, rules requiring separation of prisoners by age or sex may mean that they are kept in solitary confinement In this type of system, any attempt to classify prisoners according to their special needs is foreclosed."[3]

In England between 1945 and 1978 the prison population increased from about 12,000 to 42,000—a figure which would place the prison system in what Mr. Roy Jenkins, the then Home Secretary, said in 1975, "a state of crisis".[4] The Report of Justice May Committee[5] records that on 1 July, 1979 the certified normal accommodation (CNA) of the prison system in England and Wales was 37,881 and the number of prisoners 40,885. Nowhere in the May Report is there any discussion of the meaning of CNA but the initial assumption, according to King and Morgan, is that the system is at least 12 per cent overcrowded, and the need to keep a porportion of places vacant for receptions and transfers and other operational purposes may mean that the real level of over-crowding, as experienced by prisoners, is very much higher.[6] Insufficient accommodation apart, less than a quarter of the existing accommodation is twentieth century purpose-built, and the system is now in such a state of decay and the backlog of replacing obsolete prisons so great that even if it were possible to replace one every two years, beginning in 1980, the last Victorian prison would not be phased out until 2060.[7]

In Indian prisons too, overcrowding is a chronic problem. As far back as the late 50s, the All India Jail Manual Committee made the following observation :

> Almost all over India overcrowding in prisons has become a common problem. In some prisons the cells and barracks which were originally meant for accommodating inmates have been converted into store-rooms, godowns, work-shops, etc. The original authorized accommodation of an institution is thus slowly shrinking whereas the daily average population and the total admissions indicate a steady increase. As a consequence, overcrowding has

assumed the proportions of a major problem for the Correctional Administration. This problem presents special difficulties especially when there is a sudden influx of prisoners during socio-political agitations. On such occasions all minimum standards of institutional management virtually collapse.[8]

The Report of the Working Group of Prisons (1972-73) recorded an increase of nearly 37 per cent in the total annual admissions to prisons in 15 States and 2 Union Territories during the decade 1961-70. From 10,05,896 in 1961 the total admissions rose to 13,78,657 in 1970 and this increase was spread over most of the States and Union Territories.[9] In recent time, Justice Mulla Committee on Jail Reforms also records that conditions of living in most of the prisons in India were *sub-human* because of overcrowding of inmates and dilapidated condition of prison buildings which rendered sanitary conditions and the state of personal hygiene extremely difficult.[10] "In some of the States", as this Committee observes, "prison barracks are so overcrowded that inmates have to sleep in shifts . . . The frequent influx of large number of agitators further worsens the situation and aggravates the problem of prison management."[11] The Committee was particularly perturbed with "periodic but acute" problem of overcrowding in the sub-jails. According to its estimates, of the 1220 institutions run by the prison department of various States and Union Territories in India as many as 822 or 67.4 per cent were sub-jails with a daily average population of 19,900 inmates. The Committee is of the view that the application of the concept of daily average population to this large number of small institutions having a total sanctioned capacity of 26,057 is apparently 'deceptive'; for, the sub-jails catered mainly for undertrial prisoners whose population is constantly changing and their annual turnover is considerably larger than what the average daily population suggests. Moreover, the sanctioned capacity of these institutions is not calculated by State prison departments according to the standards of per-prisoner space laid down in jail manuals, and it has relevance only to the number of inmates traditionally locked up in them. Even at that, the sub-jails of at least four States suffer from "constant and serious overcrowding" as may be observed from Table 1 reproduced from the Committee's Report.

TABLE 1

Variation between Sanctioned Capacity and Daily Average Population in the Sub-jails of Bihar, Nagaland, Tamil Nadu and West Bengal

State	No. of sub-jails	Sanctioned capacity	Daily average population	Variation
Bihar	28	2506	3262	+1056
Nagaland	5	120	150	+ 30
Tamil Nadu	119	3662	3775	+ 92
West Bengal	31	1572	2645	+1073

Source : Govt. of India : Ministry of Home Affairs, Report of the All India Committee on Jail Reforms, 1980-83, Vol. 1, p. 224.

Causes of Overcrowding

As in many other countries, the principal causes of overcrowding in Indian prisons are unnecessary detention of undertrials and the heavy influx of short-terms convicts. As a consequence of unnecessary detention, undertrial prisoners constitute bulk of India's prison population. Justice Mulla Committee[12] records that while the total prison population in India has shown a declining trend over the past few years the ratio of undertrial prisoners per hundred of convicted prisoners went up to 149 as on December 31, 1980, and to 160 as on June 30, 1981 as may be seen from Table 2. Figures 2 and 3 based on this Table show that despite the declining trend of prison population the proportion of undertrials to the total prison population has constantly been well over 50 per cent during 1975-80, and rose up to 61.5 per cent as on June 30, 1981. The Seventh Finance Commission found this proportion to be very high in several States such as Assam, Bihar, Orissa, Uttar Pradesh and West Bengal, and in some cases it rose to as much as 80 per cent of the total inmate population.[13]

Figure 2
Declining Trend of Prison Population in India on Different Dates During 1975–81

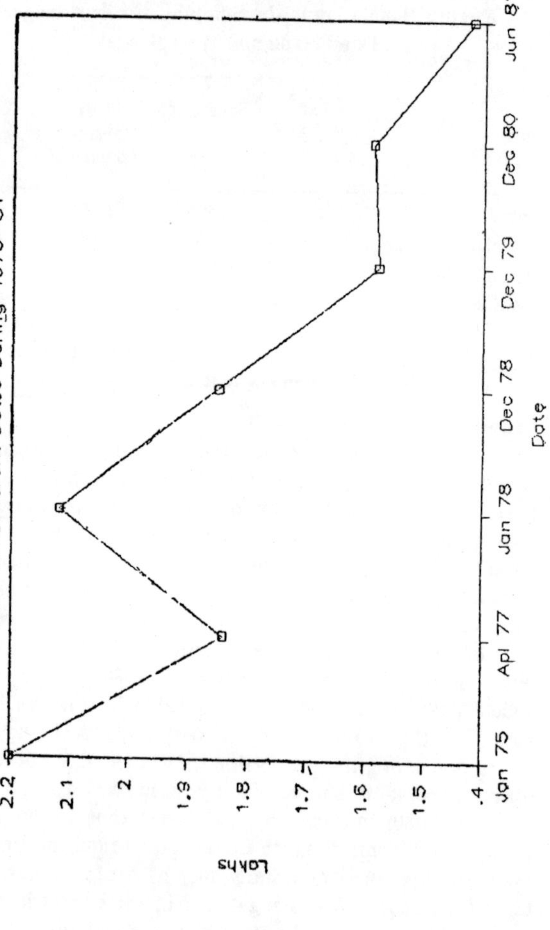

Figure 3
Percentage of Convicts & Undertrials in India on different dates during 1975–81

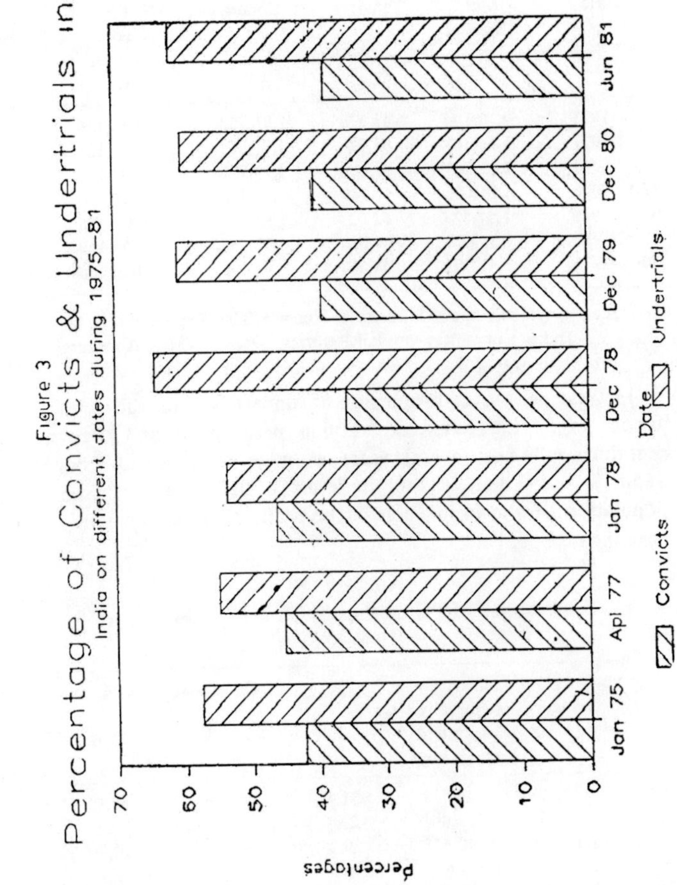

TABLE 2

Distribution of Prison Population in India on Various Dates During 1975-81

Date	Total Inmates	Convicts	Undertrials	Ratio of convicts to undertrials
1- 1-1975	2,20,146	93,374	1,26,772	100 : 136
1- 4-1977	1,84,169	83,086	1,01,083	100 : 122
1- 1-1978	2,11,963	98,186	1,13,777	100 : 116
31-12-1978	1,85,655	66,319	1,19,336	100 : 180
31-12-1979	1,57,824	62,023	95,901	100 : 154
31-12-1980	1,59,692	64,090	95,602	100 : 149
30- 6-1981	1,41,761	54,617	87,144	100 : 160

Source : Govt. of India : Ministry of Home Affairs, Report of the All India Committee on Jail Reforms, 1980-83, Vol. I, Annexure XII-A, p. 178.

In West Bengal the proportion of undertrials to the total prison population has been varying between 68 and 75 per cent during the past several years as may be observed from Table 3 and Figure 4, and in terms of daily average prison population as shown in Table 4, the proportion has constantly been over 71 per cent.

TABLE 3

Distribution of Prison Population in West Bengal (1980—85)

Year	Total Inmates	Convicts (directly admitted to prisons)	%	Undertrial	%
1980	1,29,298	40,537	31.4*	88,761	68.6*
1981	1,33,529	39,401	29.5	94,128	70.5
1982	1,37,846	40,435	29.3	97,411	70.7
1983	1,31,782	40,643	30.9	91,139	69.1
1984	1,20,171	29,988	25.0	90,183	75.0
1985	1,28,623	39,812	31.0	88,811	69.0

* Percentage figures rounded off to the nearest whole-number.

Source : Prisons Directorate, Govt. of West Bengal.

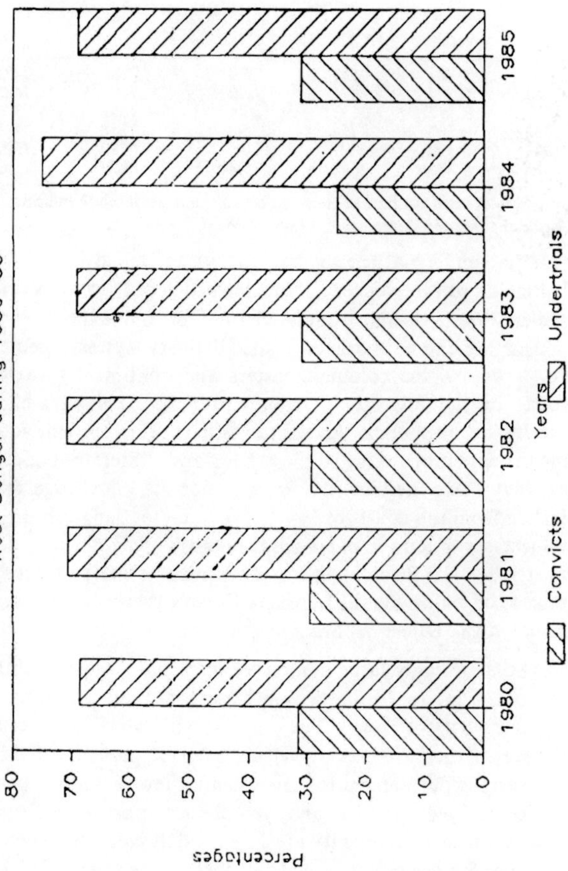

Figure 4
Percentage of Convicts & Undertrials in West Bengal during 1980–85

TABLE 4

Daily Average Number of Convicts and Undertrials in West Bengal during 1980—85

Year	Total Inmates per day (average)	Convicts	%	Undertrials	%
1980	9,701	2517	26.0*	7184	74.0*
1981	10,154	2674	26.0	7480	74.0
1982	9,992	2633	26.4	7359	73.6
1983	10,302	2654	25.8	7648	74.2
1984	9,134	2422	26.5	6712	73.5
1985	9,322	2643	28.4	6679	71.6

* Percentage figures rounded off to the nearest whole-number.
Source : Prisons Directorate, Govt. of West Bengal.

The undertrial prisoners consisting mostly of people belonging to the weaker or under-privileged sections of the society are the unfortunate victims of our expensive, time-consuming and elite-orieted justice-delivery system, bequeathed to us by the colonial masters and continued to exist till today in the interests of "an entrenched few"—the elites of the Indian Republic. Access to justice in this system actually means denial of justice to these poor and illiterate undertrials as they have neither the means nor the knowledge to seek justice from the courts of law. They are to languish in jails unnecessarily long in *many cases* because of "notorious delay" in trials and their inability to furnish necessary security for release on bail. As the Supreme Court observed in *Hussainara Khatoon and Others vs. State of Bihar*[14] :

> An alarmingly large number of men and women, children including, are behind prison bars for years awaiting trial in courts of law. The offences with which some of them are charged are trivial, which even if proved, would not warrant punishment for more than a few months, perhaps for a year or two, and yet these unfortunate forgotten specimens of humanity are in jail, deprived of their freedom, for periods ranging from three to ten years . . . and a few of them, even more than 10 years, without their trial having begun. What faith can these lost souls have in the judicial system which denies them a bare trial for so many

years and keeps them behind bars, not because they are guilty, but because they are too poor to afford bail and the courts have no time to try them. It is a *travesty of justice* that many poor accused, 'little Indians' are forced into long cellular servitude for little offences because the *bail* procedure is beyond their meagre means and trials don't commence and even if they do, they never conclude.

A Tour Note of the National Police Commission (December 1978)also speaks a volume about the plight of undertrials in India. Referring to some of the prisons as "true exponents of a system which is slowly grinding thousands of people into dust" this Note records :

> The undertrials consist of large variety of persons. Hundreds of them are dumb, simple persons, caught in the web of the law, unable to comprehend as to what has happened, what the charge against them is, or why they have been sent to jail. These are the people without a calendar or a clock, only a date in a court dairy, extended from hearing to hearing . . . there are girls sent to jail because the *Ashram* had to be closed down after some sort of scandal and several girls run away, and they are now kept in the jail in "protective custody", tearful, unwilling, and positively wanting no protection at all. Then there are more of them charged with ticketless travel, possession of weapons, or illicit liquor or some minor infraction of the law . . . A cause of concern for any student of law is the fact that several of them have been undertrials for more than five years.[15]

Unnecessary detention of undertrials apart, another principal cause of overcrowding in Indian prisons is the heavy influx of short-term convicts. A large number of these convicts usually consists of first offenders involved in technical or minor violations of law. "Such offenders, by and large", observes Justice Mulla Committee on Jail Reforms, "need no incarceration from reformative point of view. However, in spite of various provisions in law, such as probation, for diversion of such offenders from institutional treatment to treatment in the open community they continue to be sent to

Figure 5
Percentage Distribution of Convicts
acording to length of sentence in West Bengal

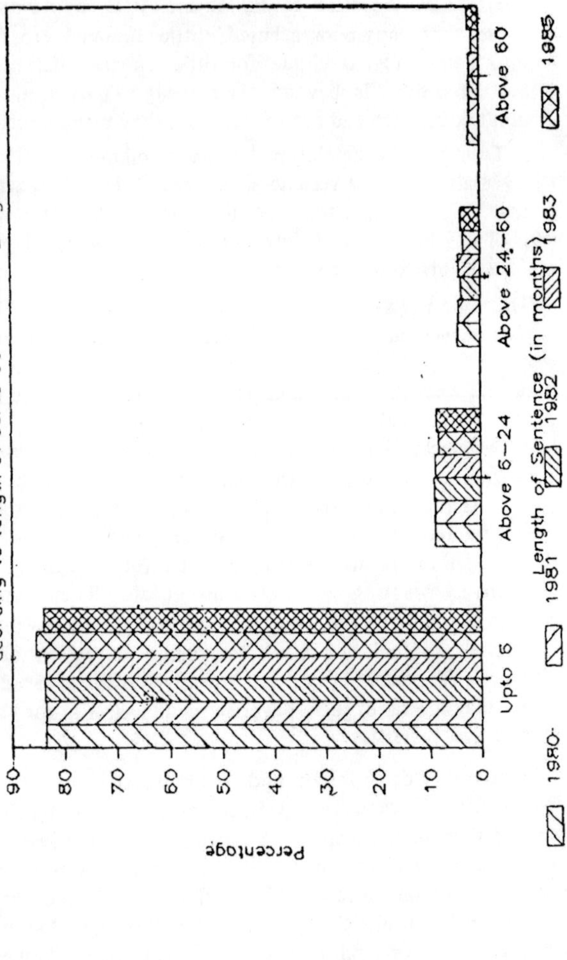

prisons in large numbers".[16] Table 5, reproduced from this Committee's Report, shows that of 59,586 convicts sentenced to rigorous imprisonment of varying lengths in India as on December, 31, 1980, 31.61 per cent undergo prison sentence for a short duration not exceeding one year. In some states, as for instance in West Bengal, the percentage of short-term convicts is much larger than the national figure. Table 6 and Figure 5 show that between 1980 and 1985, the convicts having prison sentence not exceeding 6 months constantly constitute more than 83 per cent of the total convicted prisoners in West Bengal.

TABLE 5

Distribution of Convicts Sentenced to Rigorous Imprisonment by Length of Sentence in Indian Prisons as on December 31, 1980

Length of Sentence	No.	%*
Up to 6 months	8064	13.53
More than 6 months up to 1 year	10776	18.08
More than 1 year up to 3 years	5307	8.91
More than 3 years up to 5 years	4339	7.28
More than 5 years up to 7 years	3263	5.48
More than 7 years up to 10 years	1823	3.06
More than 10 years up to life imprsionment	26014	49.66
TOTAL	59586	100

* Percentage figures rounded off to the nearest whole-number.

Source : Govt. of India : Ministry of Home Affairs, Report of the All India Committee on Jail Reforms, 1980-83, Vol. I, p-20.

Closely allied to the problem of short-term sentence is the problem of imprisonment in default of fines. Section 388 of the old Code of Criminal Procedure (1898) put "unnecessary restrictions" by limiting the payment of fine to three instalments only and the maximum time for payment, even in appropriate cases, to 60 days only. Surprisingly, these provisions have been retained in verbatim under Section 424 of

TABLE 6

Classification of Convicts Admitted Directly and also Received by Inter Jail Transfer according to their Length of Sentence in West Bengal (1980-85)

Length of Sentence	1980		1981		1982		1983		1984		1985	
	No	%*	No	%*	No	%*	No	%*	No	%*	No	%*
Not exceeding 6 months	34,725	83.60	33,486	83.59	34,335	83.73	34,665	83.60	25,690	85.30	33,425	83 92
Above 6 months and not exceeding 2 years	3,653	8.80	3,563	8.89	3,729	9.09	3,649	8.80	2,455	8.15	3,458	8.68
Above 2 years and not exceeding 5 years	1,877	4.52	1,677	4.19	1,587	3.87	1,802	4.35	969	3.22	1,484	3.73
Above 5 years	865	2.08	772	1.93	837	2.04	768	1.85	433	1.44	835	2.10
Life sentence	414	1.00	562	1.40	518	1.27	579	1.40	570	1.89	626	1.57
TOTAL :	41,534	100	40,060	100	41,006	100	41,453	100	30,117	100	39,828	100

* Percentage figures rounded off to the nearest whole-number.

Source : Prisons Directorate, Govt. of West Bengal.

the amended Code of Criminal Procedure, 1973. "Even as it is", says Dr. B.K. Bhattacharya very aptly, "the ignorance of poor undefended accused persons and the apathy (as also the reluctance) of magistrates tend to make the application of the provisions rare".[17]

Evil Effects of Overcrowding in Prisons

In a prison-setting the effects of overcrowding on inmates and institutional environment are deleterious, destructive and dehumanizing. Overcrowding is injurious not only to the morale of the prisoners but also to their health and mind. It creates a lot of problems for prison management, make custodial surveillance extremely difficult and thereby indulges such immoral practice as homosexuality. Although the victims of homosexual assaults in prisons are, in most of the cases, the young or adolescent inmates, the general effects are perhaps even more destructive than the effects that in such incidents have on the victims themselves. For, homosexual assault or "rape", as it is described by an American scholar, "impacts all prisoners and fundamentally alters the social climate of correctional institutions".[18]

The deleterious effect of overcrowding on prisoners' health is evident from the fact that the skin and other infectious diseases tend to grow. During his visit to some prisons in West Bengal this writer came across many prisoners suffering from these diseases.

Overcrowding adversely affects the prisoner's mind too. Turbulence in human mind hastens the commission of crimes. Every prisoner needs isolation, more or less, so as to be relieved of mental tension. Isolation for each of the so many prisoners means more accommodation. The more the state of overcrowding the greater is the chance of the growth of evil passions acquiring ascendancy in the minds of the prisoners. Moreover, the sense of privacy is the basis of human dignity. If a prisoner is deprived of privacy altogether, he is bound to become a thoughtless and shameless person. Consequently, any endeavour to bring about a change in his mind for reclamation becomes a difficult job for prison officials.

These apart, there are other evil effects of overcrowding in prisons. Referring to them the Report of the All India

Jail Manual Committee of 1957-59 observes: "Owing to a continuous state of overcrowding minimum standards for housing and equipment, sanitary services, water-supply, segregating inmates of various categories, etc., cannot be properly maintained; unemployment and idleness increase in prisons; discipline becomes a complicated problem; attention to the care, welfare and training of inmates becomes a difficult proposition. The overall efficiency of an institution thus getslowered."[19]

Consequences of Unnecessary Detention of Undertrial Prisoners

Unnecessary detention of undertrial prisoners often lead to "grave consequences", particularly for those who are poor and illiterate. In *Hussainara Khatoon's case*,[20] the Supreme Court pointedly mentioned such consequences as under:

(1) though presumed innocent, the poor undertrials are subjected to psychological and physical privations of jail life;

(2) they are prevented from contributing to the preparation of their defence;

(3) they lose their job, if they have one, and are deprived of an opportunity to work to support themselves and their family members with the result that the burden of their detention almost invariably falls heavily on the innocent members of the family.

Unnecessary detention of undertrials has far-reaching implications not only for the prisoners themselves but for society as well. As Dr. B.K. Bhattacharya has observed very poignantly: ' The longer the period of detention the greater is the risk of contamination of innocent undertrial prisoners by hardened criminals. It also leads to enforced idleness and sets a bad example to others, apart from the increased cost of running the jail. The undertrial prisoners feel demoralized, a sense of bitterness and collousness is aroused, and some of the prisoners may come to cherish vindictive ideas against society".[21] Again, the mixing up of inmates arrested during socio-political and economic agitations with undertrial and convicted prisoners, which has been a common feature of Indian prisons since long, adversely affects the discipline in prisons and morals of prison personnel. "Such situations", observed Justice Mulla Committee, "have often led to serious complications and mass agitations in prisons. If prisons have to function as centres of regeneration and correctional treatment, overcrowding and sudden influx of agitators in regular prisons will have to be effectively checked". Otherwise, as this Committee has warned forthrightly, "the problem of administration and management of prisons will assume such enormous dimensions that a time may come when the entire prison system might have to face a situation of total collapse".[22]

It is, therefore, clear that any scheme for correction of the prisoner without adequate housing for him is like Hamlet without the Prince of Denmark.

Evil Effects of Short-term Imprisonment

Short-term prison sentence is a harmful method of dealing with offenders from the penological as well as the sociological points of view. Prisoners with short-term sentence often get an opportunity of mixing with the hardened long-term convicts including the recidivists as a result of which they are most likely to become further debased and lose fear of imprisonment which is supposed to be the most effective deterrent to crime. A tendency to commit further crimes is thus developed in them. Reformation of this class of prisoners is next to impossible as they cannot be brought under any programme of reformatory treatment during their short stay in prison. On the contrary, they are to suffer from the social stigma of imprisonment, however short their imprisonment may be. Dr. B.K. Bhattacharya, therefore, rightly believes that short-term sentences, beyond having a *nuisance value*, accomplish little. "The offenders", he says, "is degraded and humiliated and nothing more. Extra pressure is unnecessarily put on jail population, and consequently on the jail officers. Prisons have to be extended and cost of new buildings alone will be an effective check to any internal improvement in the interest of prisoners".[23] It is of utmost importance, therefore, to consider the possibility of eliminating short-term prison sentence and substituting other alternatives in its place.

Measures for Reduction of Prison Population

Reduction of prison population must be the starting point of any programme concerning improvement of living conditions in prisons. The persistent problem of overcrowding in Indian prisons has now assumed such "gigantic" proportions that it needs to be dealt with on several fronts and in different the sectors of the criminal justice system legislature, and the judiciary.

(i) Existing Law : Application and Amendment

The re-enacted Criminal Procedure Code, 1973 has, no doubt, removed some of the earlier ambiguities about the undertrials. This Code[24] provides that—

1. For non-completion of police investigation, no Magistrate shall authorise the detention of an accused person in custody for a total period exceeding ninety days where the investigation relates an offence punishable with death, imprisonment for life or imprisonment for a term of not less than ten years, and sixty days, where the investigation relates to any other offence, and, on the expiry of the said period of ninety days, or sixty days, as the case may be, the accused person shall be released on bail.
2. The period spent by an undertrial in jail is to be counted towards the sentence which may ultimately be awarded by the court.
3. The period of detention in jail during remand is also to be counted against the sentence of imprisonment.
4. Limitation period for criminal prosecution has for the first time been prescribed and prosecutions cannot be launched thereafter except when the court for special reasons grants extension of time. The period is six months for offences punishable with imprisonment for not exceeding one year, and three years for offences punishable with imprisonment for not exceeding three years.

The re-enacted Code of Criminal Procedure has further included certain important provisions to facilitate expeditious disposal of pending cases. Trial by jury has been abolished.

Scope of summary trial has been widened by including within it offences punishable with imprisonment not exceeding two years.[25]

Finally, the 1973 Code sought to liberalize, albeit partially, stringent bail provisions of the earlier Code. Section 440 (1) of this Code, for instance, provides that the amount of every bond shall be fixed with due regard to the circumstances of the cases and shall not be excessive. Sub-section (2) of this section empowers the High Court or Court of Session to direct that the bail required by a police officer or Magistrate be reduced. Anticipatory bail may be also be granted under such conditions as provided for in section 438.

However, as the Supreme Court has observed very pertinently in *Hussainara Khatoon's case*,[26] "The Code of Criminal Procedure, even after its re-enactment, continues to adopt the same *antiquated approach* as the earlier Code enacted towards the end of the last century and where an accused is to be released on his personal bond, it insists that the bond should contain a monetary obligation requiring the accused to pay a sum of money in case he fails to appear at the trial. Moreover, as if this were not sufficient deterrent to the poor the courts mechanically and as a matter of course insists that the accused should produce sureties who will stand bail for him and these sureties must again establish their solvency to be able to pay up the amount of the bail in case the accused fails to appear to answer the charge. This system of bails operates very harshly against the poor and it is only the non-poor who are able to take advantage of it by getting themselves released on bail."

The Supreme Court, therefore, emphasized forthrightly the need for a "drastic change" in the existing bail system through liberal application of the present law and its appropriate amendments. In this context, it suggested that—

(1) instead of risk of financial loss, other relevant considerations such as family ties, roots in the community, job security, membership of stable organizations etc., should be the determinative factors in grant of bail and

the accused should in appropriate cases be released on his personal bond without monetary obligation ;

(2) It may be necessary in such a case to provide by an amendment of the penal law that if the accused wilfully fails to appear in compliance with the promise contained in his personal bond, he shall be liable to penal action ;

(3) even under the law as it stands today the courts must abandon the antiquated concept under which pretrial release is ordered cnly against bail with sureties, and that the new insight into the subject of pretrial release which has been developed in socially advanced countries and particularly the United States should now inform the decisions of our Courts in regard to pretrial release ;

(4) if the court is satisfied, after taking into account, on the basis of information placed before it, that the accused has his roots in the community and is not likely to abscond it can safely release the accused on his personal bond, and that to determine whether the accused has his roots in the community which would deter him from fleeing from justice, the court should take into account such factors concerning the accused as the length of his residence in the community, his employment status, history and financial condition, etc.[27]

The Law Commission of India, in its 78th Report, recommended *inter alia* following measures[28] for liberalization of the bail system in order to deal effectively with the large number of undertrial prisoners :

1. Expansion of the Category of Bailable Offences

(a) Certain offences under the Indian Penal Code, viz., personating a public servant (Sec. 170), criminal breach of trust (Sec. 406), offences relating to counterfeit coin (Secs. 233, 235, 237, 241, 242, 246), offences relating to corruption in public offices (Secs.161-165), etc., which are at present non-bailable, should be made bailable, and the code of Criminal Procedure, 1973, First Schedule, Part I, should be amended accordingly.

(b) Offences under laws other than the IPC punishable with 3 years' imprisonment should be made bailable with the exception of offences under the Official Secrets Act, 1923, and the Cr. P.C., 1973, First Schedule, Part II, should be amended accordingly.

2. Amount of Bond

(a) The statutory requirement that the amount of bond shall not be excessive (Sec. 440 (1), Cr. P. C., 1973) should be observed.

(b) There is no need to impose a statutory ceiling on the amount of bail.

Speedy Disposal of Cases

In Hussainara Khatoon's case, the Supreme Court observed : "Speedy trial is of the essence of criminal justice and there can be no doubt that delay in trial by itself constitutes denial of justice."[29]

Problems pertaining to 'Delay and Arrears in Trial Courts' have been dealt with at length by the Law Commission of India in its Seventy-seventh Report (November 1978). Having analysed the causes of delay in criminal trials, the Commission suggested *inter alia* the following important measures : [30]

1. Section 326, Cr. P.C. 1973 should be amended to enable a Sessions Judge to act on evidence partly or wholly recorded by his predecessor.
2. At least two police officials at every police station should be set apart for getting service of summonses effected upon witnesses for cases relating to that police station and for ensuring their presence on the date of hearing.
3. Officials at the police station who are concerned with investigation should concentrate on investigation. As far as possible, they should not be deputed for other purposes.

4. Desirability of separating the investigating agency of the police from that dealing with law and order may have to be considered.[31] The question whether the investigating agency should not be susceptible to executive control may also need consideration.

The 78th Report of this Commission observes that for dealing with the problem of large number of undertrial prisoners implementation of recommendations made in the 77th Report is a measure of first importance. However, for cases in which the accused persons are in jail the target for their disposal, according to the 78th Report, should be four months instead of six months recommended in the 77th Report. This apart, the 78th Report suggested further measures as follows for reduction of prison population :

1. In order to prevent interested parties from prolonging pending of cases, a certain amount of strictnesss is necessary to ensure prompt disposal.
2. Trial Magistrates should furnish periodical statements of cases in which the accused are in custody and which are not concluded within the prescribed time.
3. In times of agitation, numerous persons defy law and court arrest, causing a sudden spurt in the number of undertrial prisoners. Most of them would not offer bail. Such persons should be put up for trial soon after their arrest in order to avoid congestion in jails.
4. Where the accused is in jail, adjournment of cases should not be granted unless absolutely necesary.[32]

(iii) Restructuring of the Judicial System

The problem of delay in trials is by and large the product of our existing judicial system. The problem of 'system' delay, according to the Law Commission of India headed by Justice H.R. Khanna, is "the product of too much court business for too few judges, creating an imbalance in their work-time relationship". "More precisely", as this commission has further explained, "system delay occurs when the demand made by a group of cases for courtroom processing exceeds the supply of court resources, namely, judge time, available to process them.

A remedy that works is one that restores equillibrium by favourably adjusting the balance."[33] This means the appointment of more judges which seems to be nothing more than a temporary remedy, or what justice D.A. Desai says, "tinkering at the fringes". The stupendous problem of 'system' delay actually calls for thorough overhauling of our alien judicial system through many-pronged reforms which include *inter alia* simplification of court procedures, framing of detailed legislation including amendments to the antediluvian Evidence, Act, creation of National Judicial Service, imparting adequate initial and in-service training to the officers of National Judicial Service, ensuring people's participation in the administration of justice with the reinduction/revitalisation of our historically popular institution of *Nyaya Panchayat* and imparting initial training to the *Panchayat Raj* Judges and other members of the panel, i.e., the lay Judges, providing free legal services effectively to the poor and needy litigants as directed under Article 39A of the Constitution of India. The present Law Commission of India, headed by Justice D.A. Desai, has already submitted to the Government a number of voluminous reports[34] containing detailed recommendations for restructuring of judicial system. It is yet to be seen whether these valuable reports will be getting dust as usual or our ruling elites will take the desired initiative to implement them so as to save our judicial system from catastrophe.

(iv) Liberal use of Alternatives to Short-term Sentences

A very effective way of reducing the number of short-term convicts in prisons is for the courts to use the statutory provision of fines more liberally instead of passing short-term sentences. There is no doubt that fines for minor offences often meet the ends of justice, and if there be any sentence of imprisonment for a minor offence, the convict, as suggested by the West Bengal Jail Code Revision Committee of 1972-73, should be given an opportunity to serve it out of jails in public work centres instead of being sent to a regular prison to swell its population. In urban areas such an offender may be made to work on municipal roads and other works of public utility, while a petty railway offender like a ticketless traveller may be sent to work on the railway track, the goods-shed or the workshop as the case may be. If he be a tough and recalcitrant fellow and refuse to do the assigned work he may be sent to a regular prison.[35]

(v) Restricted Award of Imprisonment in Default of Fines

In a poor country like ours, prison population may be substantially reduced by imposing certain legal restrictions on the award of imprisonment in default of fines. In order that prisons may not be overcrowded with offenders who are unable to pay fines, Dr. B.K. Bhattacharaya has suggested that the trying courts should consider the ability of the offenders to pay fine. According to him, the Swedish plan of applying two different scales while imposing fines, one according to the gravity of the offence and the other according to the economic conditions of the offender, may be usefully adopted with this modification that consent of the offender may be taken before the second course is adopted in order to avoid, what Dr. Herman Manheim says, "an undersirable betrayal of financial status".[36]

(vi) Non-Institutional Treatment of Offenders

Another effective means for keeping down the number of prison population is the non-institutional or community-based treatment of offenders. In developed countries emphasis is now being given to the extensive use of probation, parole and other non-institutional techniques of dealing with both adult criminality and juvenile delinquency with the help of voluntary agencies. The experience of these countries reveals that there is ample scope for work by voluntary agencies in non-institutional treatment of offenders. Voluntary agencies, for instance, can help in application of probation by setting up Societies and Homes for the rehabilitation of probation cases. The members of these organizations may also function as Voluntary Probation Officers. Under Section 13(1)(b) of the Probation of Offenders Act, 1958 a person provided for the purpose by a 'Society' recognized in this behalf by a state government can be appointed as Probation Officer. Unfortunately, most of the state governments have not so far evinced much interest to utilize the services of Voluntary Probation Officers. As Justice Mulla Committee[37] have very poignantly observed: "The Indian probation system is seriously handicapped for want of adequate number of departmentally paid probation officers and this deficiency can be effectively remedied by utilizing the services of voluntary workers". Voluntary women organizations will be particularly helpful and effective in dealing with female probation cases.[38] Other devices like premature release and parole, if effectively utilized, may also help in reducing the number of prison population.

Conclusion

A fairly ideal accommodation in prison implies an accommodation which is conducive not only to safe custody of prisoners but also to their correctional treatment and maintenance of basic minimum standards of human dignity. In the present era of individualized training and treatment of offenders the utilities of providing separate accommodation for different categories of prisoners can hardly be denied. The problem of overcrowding in prisons, however, is a great stumbling block not only to the efficient management of prisons but also to the effective implementation of any programme aiming at improvement of living conditions in prisons. There is hardly any doubt too that in a prison-setting the effects of overcrowding on inmates and institutional environment are deleterious, destructive and dehumanizing. Although prison-overcrowding is almost a universal phenomenon, it is perhaps more menacingly prevalent in developing countries as ours. As a matter of fact, the persistent problem of overcrowding in Indian prisons has now assumed such "gigantic" proportions that it needs to be dealt with on several fronts as discussed in this chapter. The valuable recommendations of the Law Commission of India and of other official commissions and committees have also been discussed. If these are implemented, it is believed that not only the jail population will be gradually reduced, the possibility of improving the living conditions and character of those who still remain in jails will also be much enhanced. While implementation of some of these recommendations may not involve much expenditure, finance is actually the steel framework within which most of the schemes pertaining to reduction of prison population and improvement of living conditions in prisons are to be effected. Hence, while formulating any such scheme, our prison administrators and policy-makers should always take into account various retarding factors including costs in terms of time, money and skill.

NOTES AND REFERENCES

1. Sue Titus Reid, *Crime and Criminology*, 4th edn., 1985, p. 519.
2. "What Are Prisons For ? No Longer Rehabilitation, but to Punish—And Lock the Worst Away", *Time*, September 13, 1982, p. 38 ; see also Sue Titus Reid, *Op. Cit.*, p. 519.
3. Ronald L. Goldfarb and Linda R. Singer, *After Conviction*, 1973, pp. 88-89.
4. Peter Evans, *Prison Crisis*, 1980, p. 16.
5. Report of the Committee of Inquiry into the *United Kingdom Prison Services*, London, H.M.S.O., 1979, para 3.2.
6. Roy D. King and Rod Morgan, *The Future of the Prison System*, 1980, p. 114.
7. Peter Evans, *op. cit.*, pp. 16-17.
8. Govt. of India, *Report of the All India Jail Manual Committee*, 1957-59, para 38.
9. Govt. of India : Ministry of Home Affairs, *Report of the Working Group on Prisons in the Country*, 1972-73, para 2.2.1.
10. Govt. of India : Ministry of Home Affairs, *Report of the All India Committee on Jail Reforms*, 1980-83, (Chairman : Justice Anand Narain Mulla), Vol. I, Para 3.18, p. 21.
11. *Ibid.*, para 3.17, p. 21.
12. *Ibid.*, para 12.2, p. 170.
13. Govt. of India, *Report of the Seventh Finance Commission*, 1978, Chap. 10, para 39, p. 103.
14. AIR, 1979, S.C. 1360, at p. 1361 (emphasis added).
15. Govt. of India : National Police Commission, Tour Note No. 15, December 1978 : "The undertrials of India," K.F. Rustamji, Member ; reproduced in the *Report of the All India Committee on Jail Reforms*, 1980-83, Vol. I, p. 172.
16. Govt. of India : *Report of the All India Committee on Jail Reforms* 1980-83, Vol. I, para 3.15, p. 21.

17. B.K. Bhattacharya, *Prisons*, 1958, p. 44.
18. Bowker, Lee H., *Prison Victimization*, 1980, p. 1.
19. Govt. of India, *Report of the All India Jail Manual Committee*, 1957-59, para 39.
20. AIR, 1979, S.C. 1360, at p. 1362.
21. B.K. Bhattacharya, *op. cit.*, p. 47.
22. *Report of the All India Committee on Jail Reforms* 1980-83, Vol. I, para 9.2, p. 108.
23. B.K. Bhattacharya, *op. cit.*, pp. 41-42.
24. Vide Sections 167(2), 428 and 468.
25. Vide Sec. 260 of Cr. P.C., 1973. Under the old Code offences punishable with imprisonment not exceeding six months were only triable summarily.
26. AIR, 1979, S.C. 1360, at p. 1362 (emphasis added).
27. *Ibid.* at pp. 1363-64.
28. Law Commission of India (Chairman : Justice H.R. Khanna), *Seventy-Eighth Report on Congestion of Undertrial Prisoners in Jails*, February 1979, Chap. 9.
29. *Supra.* note 26 at p. 1365.
30. See pp. 56-57 of Commission's Seventy-Seventh Report.
31. According to a sample survey made at the instance of the National Police Commission in six States in different parts of the country, an average investigating officer is able to devote only 37 per cent of his time to investigational work while the rest of his time is taken up by other duties connected with maintenance of public order, VIP *bandobust* (arrangement), petition enquiries, preventive patrol and surveillance, court attendance, collection of intelligence, and other administrative work (see Fourth Report of the Commission, June 1980, para 27.7).
32. *Supra.* note 28.
33. *Supra.* note 28 at para 2.2.
34. For details, see *114th, 116th, 117th, 120th and 121st Reports of the Law Commission of India on Gram Nyayalaya, National Judicial Services, Training of Judicial Officers, Man-power Planning in Judiciary and A New Forum For Judicial Appointments* respectively.
35. See the Report of the Committee, pp. 33-34.
36. B.K. Bhattacharya, *op. cit.*, pp. 43-44.
37. Govt. of India : *Report of the All India Committee on Jail Reforms*, 1980-83, Vol. II, p. 261.
38. For further details on the role of voluntary agencies in non-institutional treatment of offenders, see Jaytilak Guha Roy, "Role of Voluntary Agencies in Prevention of Crime and Treatment of Offenders", *Indian Journal of Public Administration*, Vol. XXXIII, No. 3 (July-September, 1987).

5

HEALTH OF PRISONERS

The moral standard and the humanitarian outlook of a society are reflected in its jail conditions and the jail codes. A modern welfare state cannot adopt a 'hands off' attitude in regard to the requirements of physical and mental well-being of its citizens. This is more so in case of prisoners who are in the custody of the state and compelled to live, because of incarceration, under very difficult conditions—'physically crowded and uncomfortable, mentally isolated and frustrated'. Adequate care of prisoners' health is needed not merely on humanitarian grounds but for maintaining jail discipline and securing positive response from the inmates to all such measures intended to ensure their moral regeneration and social rehabilitation. Because, if the prisoners feel that the jail administration is absolutely indifferent and callous to their health requirements, they will reciprocally be indifferent to jail discipline and correctional courses.

According to the Association of State Correctional Administrators in the U.S.A., the World Health Organization's definition of health is more applicable to a confined population than to the population at large. Health has been defined by that organization as a state of complete physical, mental of energy to perform muscular and other functions. This means that the food should contain : (a) an adequate quantity of each type of nutrient, viz., protein, fat, carbohydrates, water, salt and vitamins ; and (b) adequate caloric value for maintaining the basal metabolism.

3. The degree of physical activity is the most important of the factors which determine the caloric value required. An average man having a body weight of 55 kilogram, not engaged in hard manual labour, will require about 2000 to 2400 calories ; a person doing heavy work would require not less than 2800 calories. An average woman having a body weight of 45 kilogram would require about 2400 calories ; a pregnant woman or a nursing mother should have additional calories.[2]

The West Bengal Jail Code vide Rule 1092 provides for classification of prisoners as follows for the purpose of diet :

Class I

1. All labouring adult made convicts in Division III.
2. All adult male undertrial prisoners in Division II who volunteer to work.

Class II

1. All convicts under the age of 16 years in Division III.
2. All female convicts in Division III.
3. All non-labouring convicts in Division III.
4. All Division II undertrial prisoners, both male and female, except the adult males who volunteer to work.

The choice of diet scale provides to the prisoners in terms of Rule 1094 of the Code is as follows :

Division III convicts and Division II undertrial prisoners are required to choose on first admission either the West Bengal or the Bihar scale of diet according as they are natives or resident of West Bengal or of Bihar or other western States. But they are warned at the time of their choice that subesquent change will not be allowed unless recommended by the Medical Officer. The diet scale chosen by a prisoner is recorded in his history ticket.

The following are the scales of diet sanctioned under Rule 1095 for Division III convicts and Division II under-trials :

Articles of Diet	West Bengal Diet For Bengalees and Oryas		Bihar Diet For natives of Bihar and other Western States of India	
	Class I	Class II	Class I	Class II
	Gram	Gram	Gram	Gram
For early morning meal—				
Rice	117	87	117	87
Salt	3.63	3.63	3.63	3.63
For other meals—				
Rice	583	496	292	262
Atta	—	—	292	233
Dal	146	146	146	146
Vegetable ..	233	233	233	233
Oil	18.125 mg.	18.125 mg.	18.125 mg.	18.125 mg.
Salt	25.375	25.375	25.375	25.375
Condiments ..	7.25	7.25	7.25	7.25

In addition to the above diet scales, fixed quantity of coal or fire-wood, antiscorbutics like lime juice, amchur or tamarind pulp (free of husk, fibre and seed) and condiments such as jeera or tejpata, turmeric, chillies, onion, garlic or ginger are to be issued daily to each prisoner. Under Rule 1098, the prisoners are also to be given a ration of fish or meat at the rate of 29 grams per head on alternate days at one or other of the daily meals. If recommended by the Medical Officer, this quantity of fish or meat can be doubled and 29 gram of dal per head deducted on that account. For vegetarians the Superintendent, in consultation with the Medical Officer, may provide substitutes for fish. The quantity of fish or meat allotted under this Rule may, however, be issued on alternate days or once or twice a week or on every fourth day, in accumulated quantity, according to the direction of the Superintendent.

Better diet is sanctioned under Rule 1100 for labouring convicts in Divisions I and II, particularly as it includes milk, butter and more fish or meat, as the following table shows :

'A' Diet		'B' Diet	
Items of Diet	Quantity Gms.	Items of Diet	Quantity Gms.
For early morning meal—		For early morning meal—	
Bread or atta or rice or Suji ..	117	Bread	117
Tea or cocoa or		Tea or cocoa or	
coffee ..	14.5	coffee	14.5
Sugar ..	58	Sugar	58
Butter ..	21.75	Butter	21.75
or ghee ..	14.5	Milk	58 ml.
Milk ..	58 ml.		
For other meals—		For other meals—	
Fine rice ..	467	Bread	350
or			
Atta ..	583	Atta	58
Dal ..	117	Fine rice ..	175
Vegetables ..	233	Dal	87
Potatoes ..	117	Vegetables ..	146
Meat or fish ..	117	Meat or fish ..	292
(or milk .35 lit. or vegetables 467 Gms. or eggs 2 in lieu of meat or fish)		(or eggs 2, in lieu of 117 Gms. of meat)	
Condiments ..	10.86	Condiments ..	7.25
Tamarind or lime	3.63	Tamarind or lime ..	3.63
Salt ..	29	Salt	29
Gur ..	14.5		

Mustard oil ..	29 c.c.	Jam or Jelly, or fruit at equivalent value of Jam and Jelly	14.5
Ghee 14.5 Gms. or mustard oil ..	43.5 c.c.	Mustard oil ..	14.5 c.c.
Dahi 117 Gms. or fruits (or Jam and Jelly to the equivalent value of 117 Gms. of Dahi)		Suet 29 Gms. or ghee	14.5
		or Mustard oil ..	43.5 c.c.
		Onion ..	43.5
Coal ..	930	Coal ..	930

The scale of diet for non-labouring convicts in Divisions I and II and Division I undertrials is the same as that prescribed for labouring convicts in Divisions I and II subject to the following modifications :

'A' Diet		'B' Diet	
For early morning meal—	Grams	For early morning meal—	Grams
Bread or Atta or Rice or Suji ..	87	Bread ..	87
For other meals—		For other meals—	
Fine rice ..	408	Bread ..	292
or Atta ..	467	Fine rice ..	146
Meat or fish .. (or milk 233 ml. or Egg 1 or vegetables 350 grams in lieu of meat or fish)	58	Meat or fish .. (or eggs 2 in lieu of 117 grams of meat)	175

It has been laid down in the Code that the total cost of A or B diet should not exceed Rs. 2.00 or Rs. 2.50 respectively for labouring convicts, and Rs. 1.80 or Rs. 2.00 respectively for non-labouring convicts and Division I undertrials. But It is obvious that if the prescribed diet is actually to be provided, its cost will be much higher in accordance with the market prices of the goods supplied. Moreover, the practice of classifying prisoners into Divisons I, II and III (on the basis of socio-economic status) for purposes of diet is not only violative of our constitutional doctrine of social justice but has also resulted in unnecessary problems and complications in diet administration. The West Bengal Jail Code Revision Committee (1972-73) has, therefore, rightly suggested that this practice should be abolished and in stead, there should be only one scale of balanced diet for all categories of prisoners. However, to prevent any consequential rise in cost, the Committee adds that "expert advice should be taken to make the prison diet meet the needs of all classes of prisoners without any appreciable increase incost".[3] It will not be very easy perhaps to implement this last recommendation of the Committee, but if it is carried out, undoubtedly the complexity in diet administration will to a great extent disappear.

Needless to say, the diet scales for convicts and undertrials in higher Divisions, as prescribed in the West Bengal Jail Code, are quite attractive. Even the diet scales for those in lower Divisions compare favourably with the standard of food that the average man outside prisons can pick up in our country. Speaking to newsmen soon after his release from the Tihar Jail on 28 May, 1974 when the 20-day all-India railway strike came to an end, George Fernandes remarked, "The total budget on diet in jail (for a prisoner) is twice what a railwayman can spend on an average on food".[4] And, what about the spending power of millions of poor men who have no employment or half-employed in field or factory ? Nevertheless, the statement of Shri Fernandes glaringly reveals the difference that exists between the prescribed food for prisoners and the food which the average Indian can earn for himself by his honest toil.

In reality, of course, prisoners, particularly the poor and the illiterate ones, seldom get such food as allotted to them under the Jail Code due to 'well organized' and 'systematic' corruption in our prisons. Barun Sengupta, a well-known journalist of Calcutta, who spent more than eight months in some jails in West Bengal as a MISA detenuduring Emergency of 1975-77, gave a factual narrative as to how a large quantity of the prisoners' allotted food used to be stolen by the corrupt prison officials. According to him, there are two or three stages where bulk of the prisoners' food is stolen. At the initial stage, the prisoners are deprived of a considerable part of their allotted diet which never enters the prisons while its money-value is shared by the tenderers and the higher authorities of prison management in terms of their underhand mutual agreements. At the next stage, a part of the part that enters the prison compound is stolen from the godown as well as the kitchen. The balance is then cooked or prepared from which some further quantity is again stolen at the time of actual distribution to the inmates.[5]

Almost similar narrative has been given by Kuldip Nayar, a responsible journalist of national eminence, in his book *In Jail.* Writing on corruption in notorious Tihar Jail where he was detained during Emergency, Shri Nayar observed : "Perhaps the way almost everyone, had his cut was most evident in our milk supply. It came in bulk to the main gate (*phatak*) there, enough milk for the top officials was taken out of the cans, which were then topped up with water. And as the cans moved to the wards, all those who handled them appropriated their share : again topping up with water". Quoting this and other personal observations recorded by Shri Nayar, the Supreme Court made the following comments in *Batra II* : "One wonders whether such an indictment made by an established writer had inclined the Government at least to appoint an Inquiry Commission to acquaint itself with the criminal life-style of correctional institutions".[6] Strangely enough, even in a State like West Bengal where the Marxist-led Left Front Government came to power after Emergency, no such Inquiry Commission was appointed. Does not prison justice require a 'progressive' government to take stern punitive actions against corrupt custodians of prisoners ?

There must be powerful and effective supervision-mechinery to prevent thefts in the supply and distribution of prisoners' food. Equally important is to bring about improvement in the quality of cooking for which the following recommendations have been made by West Bengal Jail Code Revision Committee of 1972-73 :

1. There should be one kitchen per 250 prisoners and a

steward should be appointed to supervise cooking in the jails. Orderly distribution of meals should also be his responsibility.

2. The present system of buying and storing pulses, etc., for the whole season should be abolished. There being little difference in the price between whole pulses and Dal, prison administration should purchase Dals instead of pulses to prevent the deterioration of quality due to long storage leading to consequent fall in the quality of the different items of cooked food.[7]

Cleanliness in the kitchen as well as the dining place cannot be overlooked, and that is why the West Bengal Jail Code has stipulated that the dining place is to be sheltered from sun and rain and protected from dust. In view of repeated complaints about the quality of cooked food, the State Government should see that these statutory instructions are actually observed instead of being mere paper-rules.

Canteens play a vital role in supplementing the diet. They are also a mark of liberalism in jail life. Unfortunately, in West Bengal no canteen facilities are provided for the prisoners. The Jail Code Revision Committee reasonably felt that there should be a canteen attached to every district and central jail, after the pattern of prison canteens in Uttar Pradesh, Punjab and Haryana.[8]

Attempts should also be made, as suggested by Dr. B.K. Bhattacharya, to relieve prisoners from night starvation by doling out some food late in the evening. "In order to break the long gap between the last meal at about 5 P.M. and breakfast next morning", as he pointed out, "an experiment was made in women's prisons in England of serving cocoa late in the evening. The evening cocoa is now practically universal. In India some such measure is called for".[9]

Dress and Bed

Adequate protection of prisoners' health also requires that their clothing and bedding should be kept neat and clean. Chapter XXXVIII of the West Bengal Jail Code contains detailed rules in this regard. Blanket, kurtas and bedding have to be boiled and washed once in every three months, and hospital clothing and bedding at short intervals, by a gang of men specially set apart for this work which has to be done ward by ward. Special kurtas and bedding are to be temporarily issued while the soiled articles are being dried, repaired or renewed. If possible, each jail is to be provided with a boiler and wringing machine for boiling and washing purposes. At least once a week, when the weather is fine, the bedding and blankets are to be aired in the sun for not less than three hours. However, in the present context of deplorable state of prison management in the country and of the general problem of overcrowding in prisons, it is difficult indeed to believe that these rules of cleanliness are observed in jails in accordance with the letter and spirit of the Code. For protecting the prisoners against diseases like Malaria and Filaria, the Jail Code Revision Committee has recommended that either mosquito nets are to be provided to them or their sleeping cells and dormitories are to be made mosquito-proof.[10]

Air and Light

The West Bengal Jail Code contains provisions[11] for thorough ventilation of the sleeping barracks and cells. If the barrack is flat-roofed, there should be ceiling ventilation and if it is gable-roofed, ridge ventilation. Roofs or ceilings should not be less than 3.96 metres high from the floor. In the sleeping barracks at least .93 square metre of ventilation area per prisoner has to be provided. In new barracks the ventilating area per head shall be half a window. It is the duty of the Superintendent of the jail and the Medical Officer to periodically note the condition of air in the barracks and sleeping wards, and take remedial measures if necessary.

It must, however, be mentioned that most of the existing prisons in India were built long ago by the British rulers. In such old prisons many cells and sleeping wards are now quite likely to become unfit for human occupation. These cells and wards should either be renovated or declared obsolete. But the greatest hindrance to such measure is again the problem of overcrowding in prisons.

Work and Working Conditions

Proper allocation of work and suitable working conditions are an important part of health care programmes in prisons. The expert advice of the psychologists and the psychiatrists will be of immense help in this matter.

Both indoor and outdoor work may be assigned to the prisoners ; but in any case, extremely hard work should be avoided. As the Model Prison Manual says, institutional work programme should aim at "promoting physical well being and proper development of the mind through intelligent manual labour".[12]

Working conditions in prisons should be transformed into such as are suitable for workers in factories and fields. The existing working conditions in most of the prisons in West Bengal compare very unfavourably even with the minimum standard of good working conditions in other free societies. Most of existing worksheds in these prisons were built as far back as in the British days and their structure was based on the punitive philosophy of prison labour advocated by the colonial rulers. The Jail Code Revision Committee has, therefore, very rightly recommended that "prison labour should be oriented under conditions which will stimulate industrious habits and create an evironment conducive to serious work. The management and organization of all kinds of prison labour, industrial or agricultural, should be like that of labour in a free community".[13]

As suggested by the Model Prison Manual,[14] the following facilities should be provided in places where prisoners work :

(i) Protection from heat, cold, rain, dust, smoke, fumes, gases and chemicals ;

(ii) Adequate ventilation and light ;

(iii) Drinking water ;

(iv) Washing and bathing facilities, spittoons, urinals and latrines ;

(v) First-aid facilities.

Games

The prisoners have a moral right to games and other

recreational facilities. As Dr. B.K. Bhattacharya says, "General lack of recreational facilities makes jail life extremely monotonous and irksome and tells on the health of the prisoner, particularly the mental health, and retards reformation".[15]

Games offer opportunities not only for social recreation but for physical exertion and relaxation too. It is, therefore, the duty of prison administration to ensure that in every jail appropriate facilities for games are provided to meet the health needs of inmates. The Model Prison Manual[16] prescribes the following for this purpose :

(a) Indoor games —Chess, draughts, carrom ;

(b) Outdoor games—Wrestling, volley ball, foot ball, basket ball, ring tennis and other suitable outdoor games ;

(c) Gymnastics —Physical culture, single and double bars, roman rings, barbell, malkhamb.

Rest

Rest is as much necessary as work for physical and mental well-being of the prisoner. The daily routine, particularly the hours of work, should be fixed in accordance with the need for rest in mind and body. The Model Prison Manual fixes the limit to prison-work as follows :

(a) For adult offenders —not more than eight hours a day ;

(b) For adolescent and women offenders —not more than six hours a day.

The manual assumes that the remaining period will be usefully utilized in educational and training activities, but the time so spent will not be counted as work period.[17]

On Sundays and also on gazetted holidays, the labouring convicts have to follow the daily routine, but their work should be comparatively less burdensome, e.g., cleaning up and tidying the jail premises. Apart from physical exercise, efforts should be made to engage them in other desirable activities as well on these days. Moreover, as directed by the Model Prison

Manual[18], a system of shifts and rotations should be established in Essential Service and Maintenance units so that prisoners working there may get one day's rest in a week. If necessary, reserve pools of workers may be built up for this purpose.

Medical Aid

The health of the prisoners depends very much upon the availability of medical aid. Since incarceration may have *deleterious* effects on the prisoner's mind, medical services should also be provided for mentally disturbed inmates. The Model Prison Manual[19] rightly states that "the object of medical administration in prisons is mainly to restore, and maintain the physical and mental health of prisoners and to keep up the general sanitation and hygiene of the institution to a satisfactory standard". To attain this object the Manual lays down that there shall be :

(i) Medical staff specially selected for prison work and arrangement should be made for imparting necessary training to them ;

(ii) adequately equipped hospital, both for men and women prisoners, with provisions for medical, surgical, dental and psychiatric services ;

(iii) adequate arrangement for taking prophy-lactic measures against infectious diseases and epidemics ;

(iv) sufficient aids in developing research, and reducing the incidence of delinquency and crime and conduct disorder.

As compared to general conditions prevailing in free society outside the prison walls, the medical services available to prisoners in our country do not seem to be unsatisfactory. To quote the All India Committee on Jail Reforms (1980-83),[20] "India with a population of 68 crores in 1981, has a doctor-person ratio of 1 : 3600. All the hosipitals and out-patient services in the country are overcrowded, and it is becoming increasingly difficult to secure adequate medical attention for the general public. Considering this sad state of affairs prevailing in the society in general, it is little relief to realize that with the availability of at least a part-time medical officer in each prison the ratio works out to 1 doctor for 500 persons". However, the quality of prison medical services has been considerably deteriorated during post-Independence period as compared to the colonial period when prison administration had, for a long time, been the responsiblity of officers of the Indian Medical Service who, with their discipline and thoroughness paid maximum attention to health care. And today, medical and health care in prisons, observes this Committee, "is inadequate, far from comprehensive, and in some places absent. The general practice at present is that Medical Officers posted in prisons are drawn from the Medical Department on deputation. They do not have a sense of belonging to the prison department. This generates in them an indifferent attitude, a feeling that the posting to the jail is a kind of punishment, a relegation to a place where there is lack of professional challenge in the work involved. This generally results in a very casual approach to the whole problem of preventive and curative medical services in jails".[21]

The West Begal Jail Code includes provisions for fortnightly weighment of every prisoner ; enquiry into the cause of his losing weight if there be such a case ; special diet, if necessary; precaution against infection of Malaria, Cholera and other such diseases ; separate hospitals for male and female prisoners, etc.[22]

However, as it generally happens in regard to their food, the poor and illiterate prisoners often complain of being deprived of proper medical facilities. This is so perhaps due to indifferent attitude of the jail authority, particularly the Medical Officers, most of whom, as Barun Sengupta points out, do not consider these prisoners as "human beings". As an instance, he referred to the system of medicine distribution in Calcutta's Presidency Jail and the Purulia Jail and said, as what he witnessed during his detention, that the middle-class prisoners in the Presidency Jail were given costly vitamin tablets and tonics even when not necessary, while a poor T.B. patient in Purulia had to go without necessary medicines.[23] So long as such corruption, indifference and injustice will continue to prevail, there can be no real improvement in prison medical services.

The West Bengal Jail Code Revision Committee very rightly said that the medical administration of jails should no longer be run with the help of medical officers drawn on loan or deputation from the State Health Services and with medicines supplied by the Central and District Medical Stores. The Home (Jails) Department and the Prisons Directorate, according to the Committee, were not getting the quality of service they expected from these doctors, Supplies of medicines from the Government. Stores were also found to be so meagre that the jails often had to purchase medicines worth lakhs of rupees from the open market. This sort of administration, observes the Committee, is bound to deprive the prisoners and the staff of timely supply of medicines and thereby encourage corruption. It, therefore, emphasized the need for evolving an entirely new policy both in the matter of reorganizing the jail medical services and in the procurement of medicines for the jails.[24]

Sanitation

Sanitary arrangements in most of the jails are extremely unsatisfactory. As the All India Committee on Jail Reforms (1980-83) observed, "Flush latrines are available in a very few prisons. In most of the prisons open basket-type latrines are still in use. Proper ratio of latrines to prisoners is not being maintained. Latrine and urinal facilities in barracks/dormitories for use at night are very inadequate. As a result, they overflow during the night. In most of the prisons latrines have not been provided in cells ; only pots are kept there for answering calls of nature. A perpetual stinking smell pervades the atmosphere of most of the prisons". For satisfactory sanitary arrangement in jails, the Committee lays down *inter alia*, the following important guidelines :

(i) The ratio of latrines to prisoners should be 1:6 ;

(ii) The system of open basket-type latrines should be discontinued, and the system of carrying night soil as headloads should be stopped forthwith ;

(iii) Flush/septic latrines should be provided in every barrack and cell ; and

(iv) Adequate number of separate urinals seould also be provided.[25]

Improved latrine and urinal facilities apart, adequate supply of drinking water and better bathing facilities, particularly in summer mid-days, should also be provided for the inmates in every jail. From the point of view of prisoners' health and hygienic care, all these matters, in fact, deserve priority consideration. If necessary, the State governments should be given financial assistance from the Centre.

Transfer of Prisoners on Grounds of Health

Humanitarianism requires that when a prisoner needs specialized medical treatment or surgical operation which cannot be adequately given or performed in the hospital of the jail where he is imprisoned, he should be transferred to another jail hospital or to a civil hospital, whichever is necessary for this purpose. Rules 1245 A and 1245B of the West Bengal Jail Code lay down the procedure for such transfer. It is desirable that the transfer should be arranged immediately, and not delayed till the last moment. On the other hand, the sick prisoners should not be kept in outside hospitals longer than is absolutely necessary.[26] It is better that the period of convalescence should be spent in the prison hospital.

Care and Treatment of Lunatic and Drug-Addicted Prisoners

One of the major problems of prison administration indubitably lies with lunatic prisoners, particularly the non-criminal lunatics (NCLs), as they are usually known in the official parlance. These NCLs are those unfortunate destitutes who are committed to prisons by the order of the Magistrate not for committing any offence but for their 'suitable custody' and 'proper care and control' under Sections 8 and 13 (1) (2) of the Indian Lunacy Act of 1912. Although this Act does not allow confinement of an alleged 'wandering' and 'dangerous' (non-criminal) lunatic in jail custody beyond the maximum period of 30 days, the fact remains that a large number of them are confined in prisons for a couple of years due to non-availability of beds in government mental hospitals. In West Bengal there are now over 1200 NCLs who for no fault of their own are rotting in jails. Some of them are there even for 20 to 25 years,[27] while at least one Anil Chunder Khasnobis is known to have been confined for a longer, if not the longest, period of over 30 years.[28] Since jail is not a place for proper treatment and care of a mental patient, and when there are at best one or two psychiatrists for over 1200 NCLs it is no wonder that "their care is left to untrained staff and other prisoners who by all accounts feel no qualms of conscience in depriving them anything more than the bare essentials".[29] Similar conditions prevail in the jails of other States and Union Territories too. As the All India Committee on Jail Reforms (1980-83) observed : "It is extremely unfortunate that lunatics lodged in jails are not only not given proper care and treatment but are forced to live in inhuman conditions. They are huddled up in small barracks or in cells under unhygienic conditions and without proper care".[30] Justice Krishna Iyer Committee on Women Prisoners has mentioned in its report submitted to the Government of India's Ministry of Human Resource Development in May 1987 that a very large proportion of women prisoners who are mentally disturbed and non-criminal are neglected and languish in prison because there is an acute shortage of psychiatrists to attend to them. Even more shocking is the lot of those mentally retarded young women who are conceived without knowing what it entails. During their visit to prisons two team from among the nine committee members came across such prisoners. There was no consesus among the committee members on a suggestion that women lunatics should be sterilised. But, the committee is against sending women lunatics to prison. Their place is in welfare homes where they can be treated.[31]

Describing the confinement of a mentally imbalanced person in jail as a "grossly inhuman act", the West Bengal Jail Reforms Committee of 1978-80, headed by Tarapada Lahiri has rightly suggested that Section 8 of the Indian Lunacy Act should be amended so that the person alleged to be a wandering and dangerous lunatic cannot be committed to the custody of any jail.[32] The committee has strongly recommended that the government set up mental hospitals where at least 2000 patients can be admitted and treated scientifically by experts. In the case of criminal lunatics who must be fully cured before they can be tried in a court of law, but may not be able to avail of treatment as provided for under Section 330 of the Cr. P.C., the committee directs the government to set up a 'miniature' hospital in a central jail where they can be properly cured in the interest of administration of justice.[33] Unfortunately, these valuable recommendations are yet to be implemented although as long as seven years have elapsed since the committee had submitted its final report to the government. May be, the report is still "under study".

No less complex is the problem of dealing with drug-addicted prisoners. Both preventive and curative measures need to be taken to solve this growing problem. As a preventive measure, the smuggling of psychoactive, soporiferous or any other kinds of habit-forming drugs into prison has to be stopped which, of course, is a very difficult task. Since drug racket operates in the jail through a large network of criminals, officials and non-officials, it cannot be stopped without stern governmental actions against corrupt officials as well as an effective machinery of internal vigilance. Alongwith such preventive measures there must have adequate arrangement for curative psychiatric treatment of drug-addicts in the jail hospital. For, a drug-addict, when deprived of drugs, is likely to suffer from mental imbalance or depression unless he gets adequate care and treatment. He may even commit suicide. In West Bengal's Dum Dum Central Jail, Shyamal Dasgupta, a young prisoner, was reported to have committed suicide on 17 June 1987, just two days after he was sent there with a short-sentence of only five days' imprisonment for ticketless train-travelling. A preliminary investigation revealed that Shyamal was a drug-addict and that he committed suicide for want of heroin. Is not such an incidence enough to justify the need for taking preventive and curative measures in respect of drug-addicted prisoners ? A negative answer is perhaps next to impossible.

Conclusion

One of the fundamental duties of prison administration is to look after the prisoners' health. The adequate care of prisoners' health requires not merely provision for medical aid but various other facilities in regard to food, dress, bed, air and light, work, games, rest, transfer of ailing prisoners to other institutions for specialized treatment and care and treatment of lunatic and drug-addicted prisoners. Various measures recommended by a number of official committees and commissions and the provisions laid down in the Model Prison Manual and the West Bengal Jail Code in regard to these facilities have been discussed and it is strongly felt that no spectecular improvement in the existing health services is really possible without efficient management of prisons in general and reorganization of medical administration of jails in particular.

NOTES AND REFERENCES

1. Association of State Correctional Administrators, South Carolina Deptt. of Corrections, Columbia : U.S.A., *Uniform Correctional Policies and Procedures*, 1972, p. 17.
2. Committee's Report, Para 186.
3. Committee's Report, p. 65.
4. *The Amrita Bazar Patrika*, May 29, 1974.
5. Vide third part of the series of articles by Barun Sengupta, *Anand Bazar Patrika*, (Bengali daily), January 24, 1977.
6. *Sunil Batra* v. *Delhi Admn.*, AIR 1980 SC 1579 at 1587 per Krishna Iyer, J.
7. Committee's Report, pp. 65-66.
8. *Report of the West Bengal Jail Code Revision Committee* (1972-73), p. 44.
9. B.K. Bhattacharya, *Prisons*, 1958, pp. 99-100.
10. Committee's Report, p. 66.
11. Vide Rule 1179 (2) and (3).
12. All India Jail Manual Committee (1957-59), *Model Prison Manual*, 1960, p. 133.
13. Committee's Report, p. 64.
14. Chap. XXIV, Rule 11.
15. B.K. Bhattacharya, *op. cit.*, p. 93.
16. Chap. XXIV, Rule 3(ii).
17. Chap. XXIV, Rule 7(i) including notes 1 and 2.

18. Chap. XXIV, Rule 10(ii).
19. p. 224.
20. Committee's Report, Vol. I, p. 82.
21. *Ibid.*, pp. 82-83.
22. For further details, see Vol. I, Chap. XL of the West Bengal Jail Code.
23. Vide the last part of the series of articles by Barun Sengupta, *Anand Bazar Patrika*, January 29, 1977.
24. Committee's Report, p. 16.
25. Committee's Report, Vol. I, pp. 74-75.
26. *Model Prison Manual*, Chap. XXXIII, Rule 8(iv).
27. Bachi J. Karkaria, "The Agony of Idleness", *The Statesman*, February 2, 1981.
28. Umesh Anand, "A Dumping Ground", *The Telegraph*, January 16, 1983.
29. *Ibid.*
30. Committee's Report, Vol. I, p. 84.
31. Promilla Kalhan, "Towards Gender Justice", *The Hindustan Times*, June 15, 1987 ; see also *Report of the National Expert Committee on Women Prisoners* (Chairman : Justice Krishna Iyer), Vol. I, Part I, Chap. IX.
32. The All India Committee on Jail Reforms (1980-83) also recommended that NCLs should not be kept in prisons and necessary amendments should be made in the law for the purpose (See Vol. I, p. 40 of the Committee's Report).
33. *Supra* note 28.

6

EDUCATION OF PRISONERS

Education is the heart and soul of the correctional process. It brings about "sublimation of the anti-social instinct in a criminal" by slowly moulding his knowledge, character and behaviour. It helps the offender in his ultimate resettlement in society. Commenting on the necessity of education and training of offenders, the Report of the West Bengal Jail Code Revision Committee (1972-73) very pertinently observes : "As reformatory treatment of criminals has been accepted as the best means of protecting society we have to bring about this reformation through a consistently humane process. And what process is more humane than the one that opens the dark recesses of a criminal's soul and admits into it, perhaps for the first time, the light of knowledge and reason ? Centuries of bitter experience tells the civilised man of today that society cannot be adequately protected only by inflicting retributory and deterrent punishment on an offender against it. It is essential, therefore, that we should seriously provide for the training and education of every criminal and endeavour seriously to develop in him a sense of self-confidence and personal responsibility."[1]

The course of education and its method must depend on

the age of the prisoner, his or her social status, occupation, general culture, past records and period of imprisonment. The education of a juvenile delinquent, for instance, is bound to be different from that of a hardened criminal. Similarly, the educational programme for a short-term prisoner needs to be different from a long-termer.

Most of the correctional activities should be woven around diversified correctional programmes in accordance with different types of crimes and degrees of malleability of the prisoners. The prison population being diverse in terms of wide variations of intelligence and interests, it is necessary, as the All India Jail Manual Committee (1957-59) very rightly felt, to orgnaize different educational programmes to suit the needs of different inmate groups.[2] While formulating such programmes, however, the prison administrators are required to pay due attention to financial constraints.

The term "education" is being used in a very broad sense in contemporary correctional programme. It includes, to quote Sutherland and Cressey, "all intentional efforts to direct inmates away from crime by means of non-academic, as well as academic, measures". From this point of view, education of prisoners is almost synonymous with "treatment of prisoners."[3] This broad conception of prison education has been more vividly expressed in the New York State Correctional Law:

> The objective of prison education in its broadest sense should be the socialization of the inmates through varied impressional and expressional activities, with emphasis on individual inmate needs. The objective of this programme shall be the return of these inmates to society with a more wholesome attitude toward living, with a desire to conduct themselves as good citizens and with the skill and knowledge which will give them a reasonable chance to maintain themselves and their dependents through honest labour. To this end, each prisoner shall be given a programme of education which . . .seems most likely to further the process of socialization and rehabilitation . . .[4]

For jail purposes, education may broadly be divided into two categories : general and vocational.

GENERAL EDUCATION

There are two main purposes of general education : (i) removal of illiteracy, and (ii) creation of a sense of social responsibility.

Emphasizing the importance of literacy to prisoners, Dr. Bhattacharya very poignantly observes : "Literacy, even elementary education, can make a world of difference specially in the lives of long-term prisoners. It is difficult for us to know what life would be like if we were illiterate and immured in prison. Even old prisoners show eagerness to be able to read and write and to get information, though some of them may feel that they are too old to learn and many are too shy to admit their ignorance. Books offer the best 'escape' outlet, and the prison school is a great stabilising factor and its therapeutic value is considerable".[5]

Removal of illiteracy however, is not a very easy task. Official statistics reveal that while literacy in India increased from 16.6% to 36.2% during 1951-81 the actual number of illiterates during the corresponding period went up from 30 crores to 42.4 crores.[6] No wonder then that, in 1971, out of the total number of 3,19,862 male and 11,493 female prisoners in the jails of 14 States and one Union Territory in India, 1,85,158 male and 8,721 female prisoners were illiterate.[7] In percentage terms, it means that 57.89% of male prisoners and 75.88% of female prisoners were illiterate. Although all-India statistics on prisons beyond this period is not available, there is no reason perhaps to assume that the situation has since then been improved. The bulk of both men and women prisoners in a major state like West Bengal, for instance, were illiterate even during the period 1980—85, as Tables 7 and 8 and Figures 6 and 7 show.

The term 'literate' in Tables 7 and 8 includes all those who are able to read and write. Dr. B.K. Bhattacharya observes that "the standard even of this limited literacy is very poor. Writing includes just being able to sign one's name, or rather 'draw' one's name, howsoever unintelligently it may be done. The real figures for literacy, therefore, are much smaller."[8]

It is unfortunate that our prisons are still operating more

Figure 6

Percentage of Literate & Illiterate

Male Convicts in West Bengal—1980–85

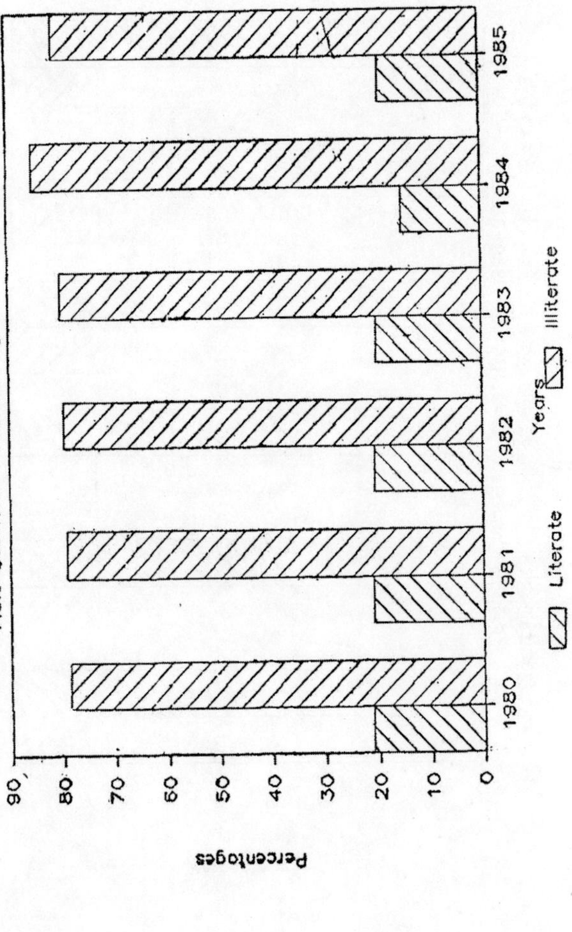

Figure 7

Percentage of Literate & Illiterate

Female Convicts in West Bengal—1980-85

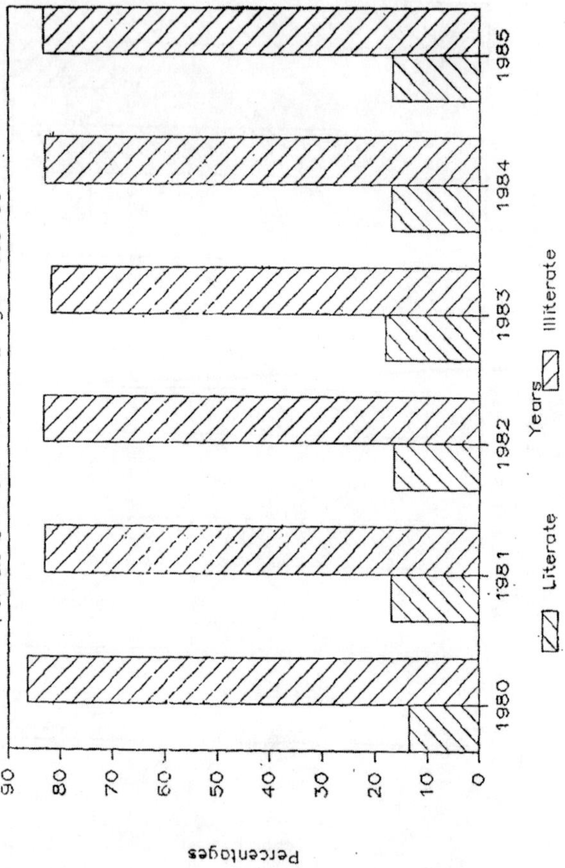

TABLE 7

Educational Level of Male Convicts in West Bengal (1980—85)

Educational	1980		1981		1982		1983		1984		1985	
Level	No	%	No	%	No	%	No	%	No	%	No	%
Literate	8,445	21.2*	7,988	20.8*	8,041	20.4*	7,983	20.0*	4,452*	14.8*	7,245	19.0*
Illiterate	31,339	78.8	30,499	79.2	31,463	79.6	31,755	80.0	25,752	85.2	30,971	81.0
Total	39,784	100	38,487	100	39,504	100	39,738	100	30,204	100	38,216	100

* Percentage figures rounded off to the nearest whole-number.

Source : Prisons Directorate, Govt. of West Bengal.

TABLE 8

Educational Level of Female Convicts in West Bengal (1980—85)

Educational Level	1980		1981		1982		1983		1984		1985	
	No	%	No	%	No	%	No	%	No	%	No	%
Literate	239	13.6*	250	16.9*	250	16.6*	331	18.2*	222	17.0*	272	16.8*
Illiterate	1515	86.4	1233	83.1	1260	83.4	1490	81.8	1083	83.0	1343	83.2
Total	1754	100	1483	100	1510	100	1821	100	1305	100	1615	100

* Percentage figures rounded off to the nearest whole-number.

Source : Prisons Directorate, Govt. of West Bengal.

as breeding places for hardened criminals than correctional institutions. A major factor responsible for this is that prison administrators have so far ignored, if not failed to even realize, the therapeutic value of education in correctional process. During his visit to Calcutta's Presidency Jail on a sweltering June day in 1974, the present researcher was astounded by a peculiar place of learning, called the "jail school". It was a classroom furnished with necessary apparatus such as black-board and benches, but the only occupant was the fulltime paid teacher relaxing in a chair. When asked about his pupils, the teacher replied casually : "The prisoners are not interested in learning". The prisoners' explanation, on the other hand, was exactly the opposite.[9] Whatsoever be the reason, it may not be very inappropriate to say that the system of imparting education to prisoners in this and perhaps in many other jails in this country is a mere farce at the cost of public money. As the Working Group on Prisons in India observed long ago : "Even after years of incarceration, many prisoners come out as illiterate as they were at the time of admission. Modern techniques of teaching adults have not found an entry into the prisons and the outmoded frustrating methods fail to arouse any enthusiasm among the prisoners. There is great scope for utilizing the talents of the educated prisoners for the instruction of the illiterate and the semi-literate. Audio-visual methods and the mass-media could also be mobilized for imparting formal education in prisons."[10]

The problem of illiteracy in the Indian prisons is further aggravated by the fact that under the Jail Codes of many States basic education is not compulsory for illiterate convicts. It would surely make a difference if every adult offender was compelled to attend a short literacy course, of three to six months' duration, comprising teaching of letters, simple words and the ability to write at least one's name and address.

Another major objective of general education in prisons is to develop in every offender a sense of social responsibility. The course on social responsibility should include basics of the nature and structure of society, for independence of its different parts, social values, necessity of law and order, the meaning and importance of democracy as a form of government from

Village Panchayets upwards, and the reasons behind punishment.

The detailed nature of the course on social responsibility has obviously to depend on the period of imprisonment, and if this period is rather short, there should be a selection of the important elements and if possible, a summary of the whole course.

Moral and Spiritual Education

The general educational programme in a prison should also include moral and spiritual education, for they all have an elevating influence. Commenting on the need of this aspect of education for shaping the minds of women offenders during incarceration, a distinguished social worker, Shrimati Sudha Mazumdar, observes : "Left to themselves, the minds of the unfortunate women who find themselves in prison upon their conviction remain unrepentant and are exposed to thoughts of anger, resentment and hatred. This makes a return to normal life and adjustment to society extremely difficult. Since the ultimate aims of penal institutions are to wean the prisoner away from wrong-doing and help her return to society as a better citizen, no matter how much is done in the way of material benefits, it will avail little if moral and spiritual welfare is neglected."[11]

Most sociologists today agree that religion is a very powerful instrument of social control and discipline and a secular democracy need not be anti-religious in its policy and administration. Under Article 28(1) of the Constitution of India, religious instruction cannot be provided in any educational institution wholly maintained out of State funds. Article 25(1), on the other hand, stipulates that subject to public order, morality and health, and to the other provisions of Part III of the Constitution, all persons are equally entitled to freedom of conscience and the right freely to profess, practice and propagate religion. Religious courses cannot, therefore, be introduced in jails compulsorily for all the inmates, since jails are governmental institutions. However, where the prisoners desire them voluntarily, adequate facilities should be available to help them in this matter. Unfortunately, although the Jail

Codes of some of the States such as West Bengal and Kerala provide for certain facilities for prayers and religious ministration for interested prisoners, there is hardly any satisfactory arrangement for imparting moral and spiritual instructions in most of the prisons in India.

Effective moral instruction is a difficult process and goes far beyond a list of "Don'ts". Epics, songs, stories and even novels in which the social malaise is very skilfully diagnosed and focussed, may be the media of such instruction. As Shrimati Mazumdar observes very aptly :

> To bring in a transformation of the (criminal's) mind, mere copy book maxims are of little use, for it is an undeniable fact that the moment a thing is forbidden the mind rebels and immediately seeks it. It is because of this all the world loves well-told stories that stimulate and sustain the spirit and teach the verieties of Life . . . To the majority of us here in India, the teachings of the ancient Epics are still vital factors of national thought. To countless numbers of our people they are very real and hold all truth and wisdom. Their faith and love for the heroes of the Ramayana and Mahabharata have withstood the test of Time and are to this day as strong as ever.[12]

This is one approach, and there are other approaches also to this great problem. However, the success of any educational programme especially in prison ultimately depends on the quality of the teaching staff. As the Report of the West Bengal Jail Code Revision Committee (1972-73) says, "The direct teaching and moralising methods of education are not likely, by themselves, to make better citizens, better workmen and better familymen. Good teachers can, however, by *suggestion* make a man look more clearly at himself and set in motion changes in attitude which can lead to a satisfactory adjustment of himself both to his family and to society at large."[13] Teachers for any educational course in prison should, therefore, be selected from among those who are known for their patience, perseverance and dedication to this sort of work.

Knowledge of Health and Hygiene

Moral and spiritual education aside, the prisoners are also required to have basic knowledge of health and hygiene. Both the All India Jail Manual Committee and the West Bengal Jail Code Revision Committee have emphasized the need of this kind of education. From the administrative and economic points of view, health or hygiene education seems more necessary for warders than for prisoners. They lack in it although they are, by the very nature of their duty, close to the prisoners. If they are given this sort of education, they would be able in their turn to offer to the prisoners necessary advice in health matters more effectively.

Cultural Education

Cultural education is expected to make a man more decent. It also helps to bring about a constructive change in his mind. Since the idle mind is indeed the devil's workshop, the prisoners should be engaged in creative activities such as music, art and drama. Such involvement not merely provides relaxation and a break from the monotony of jail life, it is also an ideal opportunity for group therapies and the personal development necessary for the correctional and socialisation process. The Art School in the Alipore Central Jail of Calcutta is an excellent example of the contribution an enthusiastic prison administrator can make to the educational programme in a prison despite financial constraints. The School was set up in 1956 by the then Suprintendent of this Jail, Mr. H.W. Shea. This devoted man was perhaps the only European administrator who continued to remain in the prison service of this State after Independence. In taking up such commendable work, Mr Shea was encouraged by his wife who was an amateur artist. There were other helpful coincidences. There was no difficulty, for instance, in finding the first instructor since Mr Debabrata Shome who was then the Discipline Officer of this Jail had a Degree in Art. The authorities were also fortunate to receive active and unstinted cooperation from a well-known artist, Mr. Pritish Dey and Mr. Biresh Bhattacharya who were then inmates of this Jail as accused in the famous Dum Dum Basirhat Conspiracy

Case of 1950. There are now about 15 students in this Art School. Their work, which is often displayed in public exhibitions, always has a good market. The money received from such sales is kept in the account of the artists and given to them at the time of release. It is interesting to note that the present Instructor received his training in art at this School while undergoing a life sentence. He was appointed part-time Instructor after his release.[14]

Facilities for Continuation of Education

Over and above programmes for general education, assistance should also be extended, as much as possible, to those inmates willing to continue their studies. The *Model Prison Manual*[15] has suggested the following facilities which may be given to prisoners for this purpose :

(i) Text books ;
(ii) Guidance of and help to the inmates preparing for examinations ;
(iii) Permission to carefully selected prisoners to appear at external examinations ;
(iv) Facilities for self-study ;
(v) Correspondence courses ;
(vi) Guided reading ;
(vii) Financial and other assistance in deserving cases at the discretion of the Superintendent.

The prison administration may also explore necessary assistance from the Open Universities to help those prisoners who do not possess the required formal degree but are willing to undertake studies in general or specialized disciplines at the undergraduate and postgraduate levels.

Library Facilities

The importance of good libraries for prison inmates to secure their mental revolution has been emphasized both in India and abroad. "A good library", observes Dr. B K. Bhattacharya, "is an adjunct to a sound educational policy. Even when poorly stocked, a prison library can be a blessing. Cellular life and long hours of enforced idleness and solitude intensify the needs of good books".[16] Almost in equal terms write Sutherland and Cressey: "In addition to affording recreational reading activities, a well-organized prison library can contribute to all phases of the educational programme. It may also serve to connect the inmate with outside, law-abiding society, and, if there is a reading room, it provides him with an oasis where, momentarily at least, he can exclude from his life the deleterious influences of the prison environment."[17]

The *Model Prison Manual*[18] lays down the following guidelines regarding the organization of a prison library:

(i) The library should provide reading opportunities of a whole-some nature. It should serve as a source of supplementary information. Books, periodicals and newspapers should be carefully selected to meet the needs of the inmates;

(ii) There should be a close integration between the library and other educational activities of the institution;

(iii) Arrangements should be made to distribute books, newspapers and periodicals to sections of the institution where inmates are housed;

(iv) The librarian should stimulate interest of inmates in reading.

TECHNICAL AND VOCATIONAL EDUCATION

Facilities for technical and vocational education should be made available to the prisoners in accordance with their age, sex, aptitude and preferences for their future rehabilitation as respectable citizens. The Report of the Advisory Council on the Employment of prisoners in England, Wales and Scotland, states: "No doubt one reason why some people follow a life of crime is that it has never been brought home to them that they are capable of doing a satisfying, honest job. Where in such cases they have the ability to do a skilled job, it is highly desirable that they should be given the necessary training. This is the purpose of vocational and industrial training in prisons. Both of these consist of courses of training in skilled trades combined with practical work, the main difference between them being that [in industrial training the practical work is done in production workshop."[19]

One of the significant social consequences of imprisonment is that it adversely affects employment or working life of prisoners after release. Available data reveal that in India a large number of persons were employed at the time they committed the offence. Though a greater percentage of prisoners coming from rural areas are cultivators, but 80 per cent of those who hail from urban areas are found to have held steady jobs at the time of their arrest. On being sentenced, these convicts lose their jobs, and on release they find it extremely difficult to get them back. Even those who manage to get in, are dismissed when their employers come to know of their criminal past.[20]

In other countries these obstacles may not be insurmountable, but still they are there. In the United States, for instance, public and employer attitudes, laws and licencing regulations bar ex-offenders from employment. As an important publication discloses : "Too often, the government which urges the ex-offender to pursue a normal law-abiding life is the same government that bars the way to that pursuit. By reason of various state statutes, certain manufacturers cannot employ convicted felons. An official of the law Enforcement Assistance Administration testifying before the Senate Judiciary Penitentiaries Subcommittee told of a man with a misdemeanour record being denied a taxi driver's license, and of a federal court upholding a city's refusal to hire an ex-convict as a tree trimmer."[21]

In view of practical difficulties for ex-offenders to secure stable and suitable jobs after release, the prisoners should be given such technical and vocational education as would enable them to establish themselves through self-employment. To achieve this end, a fresh look is necessary at our jail industries which are still largely confined to those established by the colonial British rulers who viewed work in prison "in punitive terms as a punishment for the wrong done rather than as a necessary and constructive rehabilitative tool". The alarming magnitude of the unemployment problem and the lack of sufficient economic resources in our country suggest that technical or industrial education in prisons should be imparted with an eye on labour rather than on capital-intensive industries. Cottage industries seem to be ideal for this purpose. But, as the well-known thinker on prison-reforms, Dr. B.K. Bhattacharya, observes, "Concentration on cottage industries only will not produce ultimately good results because prisoners on discharge have very little cash to carry on . . . To expect Government to provide capital to released prisoners is going too far and putting a premium on ex-convicts at the expense of good and honest citizens. Such industrial training should be given as would be useful to a prisoner after his release . . . In Jails there should be facilities for giving the men training in carpentry and smithy and in such business where not much capital is needed, such as manufacturing sealing-wax, ink, rubber-stamp, book-binding etc."[22] Tailoring, typewriting, toy making, farming and dairying, cooking, laundry and hair-dressing may also be useful. For female prisoners, there should be facilities for learning sewing, tailoring, toy and doll making, knitting and embroidery, noodles, pickles and papad making etc. Recalling the large number of undertrial women and their legal right to idle, Justice Krishna Iyer Committee on Women Prisoners recommend that the perspective of promoting work for its *intrinsic* value should be widely enforced without threatening the prisoner's rights. To achieve this, "work in prison", as the Committee observes further, "has to be given such potential economic worth and utility that all women in custody are willing to engage in work programmes."[23]

Development of prison work programmes involves considerable expenditure. But, as Justice Mulla Committee on Jail Reforms observes very pertinently: "The subject of prisons has not yet been included in the mainstream of our national development plans ; it has continued to be in the non-plan sector. It is indeed a sad reflection that the huge man-power available in prisons has not been fully utilized in the States and Union Territories for want of adequate and planned investments. It appears that the State Governments and Union Territory Administrations do not recognize that such investment will not only enhance the production of prison industries but will also be in the larger interests of the society as it would help in the resocialisation of offenders."[24]

Role of Voluntary Agencies

The western experience of correctional work reveals that voluntary agencies have a special role to play in educating prisoners. In fact, the services of these agencies can be utilized in prisons for organizing literacy programmes, health camps, programmes for moral and spiritual education, cultural and recreational activities, technical and vocational training etc. Unfortunately, in our country such voluntary services have not been encouraged or utilized by the State Governments or Union Territory Administrations to any meaningful extent.

Voluntary women organizations will be particularly helpful and effective in educating female prisoners. In the women's section of Calcutta's Presidency Jail, for instance, some voluntary agencies have been rendering invaluable, dedicated service in imparting, both general and vocational, education to prisoners. The pioneer organization in this field is the Prison Reform Committee of the National Council of Women in India, which, in addition to other programmes, have organized since 1955 *Ramnam Kirtan*, *Bhajans* and reading from the *Ramayana* twice a month on Sundays. This has proved very popular and now continues with a government grant. They have also started a nursery class for lost and stray children and those accompanying their mothers to jail. Other Voluntary organizations functioning here are the Soroptimist International of Calcutta and the All Bengal Women's Union. With cooperation from jail authorities, they have successfully taken up programmes, such as training in art and crafts, manufacture and sale of greeting cards, table-mats etc. The latest addition to these programmes is manufacturing of cigarette packets by hand-operated machines through the collaboration of a leading tobacco company. Prisoners are paid for their work too. The success of these programmes calls for an extension of voluntary services to other prisons in the country, covering both male and female offenders.[25] The Mulla Committee have also suggested *inter alia* that community groups can be organized as *Friends of Prisoners* to collect books, magazines and journals and distribute them to prison-inmates for their leisure-time reading and to organize lectures and audio-visual demonstrations in prisons on secular moral topics and on social education for the benefit of inmates.[26]

The services of voluntary women organizations may also be utilized for mainstreaming female prisoners in existing socio-economic and welfare programmes of the Central and State Governments and Social Welfare Boards by making them eligible, among other needy women, for these programmes. Justice Iyer Committee's preliminary exchanges with the Central Social Welfare Board have thrown up several possibilities of women, while in prison, qualifying for and taking advantage of the Board's schemes intended to support women and to make them self-reliant.[27] Since one of the basic procedural requirements is that grants are given to registered voluntary bodies, local voluntary women organizations which are particularly known for their honesty and dedication should be encouraged to run such programmes in prisons.

Conclusion

Education is the very base of the modern correctional process. It not only brings about sublimation of the anti-social instinct in a criminal but also helps him in his ultimate resettlement in society. An ideal scheme of prison education should include diversified programmes for both general and vocational education with emphasis on the needs of different inmate groups. Elementary education apart, the general educational programmes in a prison should also include moral and spiritual education, cultural and creative activities. Correction and change in the prisoner's mentality can be brought about if certain other facilities are extended to the deserving inmates, such as supply of books, periodicals and newspapers and facilities for continuation of studies during incarceration. In view of practical difficulties for ex-offenders to secure stable and suitable jobs after release, the prisoners should be given such vocational training as would enable them to establish themselves through self-employment. This calls for a fresh look at jail industries which are still largely confined to those established by the colonial British rulers and hardly have any bearing on the present day needs of rehabilitation. To ensure that development of prison work programmes and vocational training does not suffer for lack of funds the subject of prisons needs to be included in the mainstream of our developmental plans. The services of voluntary organizations may also be meaningfully utilized for organizing various educational and work programmes in prisons.

NOTES AND REFERENCES

1. Govt. of West Bengal : Home (Jails) Deptt., *Report of the West Bengal Jail Code Revision Committee*, 1972-73, pp. 38-39.
2. Govt. of India, *Report of the All India Jail Manual Committee*, 1957-59, para 83 and 84 (v).
3. Edwin H. Sutherland, and Donald R. Cressey, *Principles of Criminology*, 2nd Indian Reprint, 1968, p. 529.
4. *New York Correctional Law*, Chap. 864, Sec. 136.
5. B.K. Bhattacharya, *Prisons*, 1958, p. 82.
6. *Statistical Abstracts* ; *India*, pp. 539-40.
7. Govt. of India : C.B.C.S., *Social Defence* : *A Statistical Handbook*, 1976, p. 11.
8. B.K. Bhattacharaya, *op. cit.*, p. 83.
9. Jaytilak Guha Roy, "Education Behind Bars," *The Statesman*, Calcutta, August 3, 1981.
10. Govt. of India : Ministry of Home Affairs, *Report of the Working Group on Prisons in the Country*, 1972-73 (Mimeographed), p. 115.
11. Sudha Mazumdar, "Rehabilitation of Female Offenders," a paper (mimeographed) presented at the C.B.C.S., sponsored Training workshop for Correctional Services held at Calcutta on 29 March, 1974.
12. Sudha Mazumdar, *Women in Prison at Home and Abroad* (monograph), 1957, pp .28-29.
13. Report of the Committee, pp. 40-41.
14. Jaytilak Guha Roy, *op. cit.*
15. Chapter XXIII, Rule 6.
16. B.K. Bhattacharya, *op. cit.*, p. 89.
17. Edwin H. Sutherland and Donald R. Cressey, *op. cit.*, p. 540.
18. Chapter XXIII, Rule 9.
19. *Work for Prisoners*, London ; H.M.S.O., 1970, p. 19.
20. Ram Ahuja, "A Prisoner is a Human Being," *Times Weekly*, May 27, 1973.

21. *Marshalling Citizen Power to Modernize Corrections* (Monograph), Chamber of Commerce of the United States, reprinted in 1972 by the American Correctional Assocn., pp. 13-14.
22. B.K. Bhattacharya, *op. cit.*, p. 60.
23. Govt. of India : Ministry of Human Resource Development, *Report of National Expert Committee on Women Prisoners* (Chairman : Justice Krishna Iyer), May 1987, Vol. I, p. 153.
24. Govt. of India : Ministry of Home Affairs, *Report of the All India Committee on Jail Reforms* (Chairman : Justice A.N. Mulla), 1980-83, Vol. I, pp. 144-45.
25. Jaytilak Guha Roy, *op. cit.*
26. *Supra.* note 24 at p. 260.
27. *Supra.* note 23 at p. 150.

7

DISCIPLINE AND PUNISHMENT OF PRISONERS

In any prison, certain ordinary rules of discipline are necessary so that its everyday institutional life may be regulated in a manner that will make the institution an orderly, self-respecting community. If such rules are not adequately observed by the prisoners and others concerned, troubles are bound to arise sooner or later. However, the enforcement of ordinary rules of discipline in a prison is not an easy task. It is desirable, on the one hand, that the prison administrators should not have retributive or repressive attitude in maintaining discipline and, on the other, they should not be unnecessarily lenient. On this point, the *Model Prison Manual* rightly says : "Discipline and order shall be maintained with firmness, but with no more restrictions than required for safe custody and well-ordered community life. The tone of discipline should be adjusted to the requirements of each individual inmate."[1]

There should be three stages for the enforcement of ordinary rules of discipline in prisons : (i) persuasion, (ii) warning or admonition, and (iii) punishment. At the first instance, when a prisoner violates the prison rules, the jail administrators should try to make that prisoner understand the necessity of observing such rules. They should also extend their sincerest cooperation so that the prisoner can adjust himself to the routine and purpose of the institution. In case of violation of prison rules for the second time, the prisoner should be given another chance to change his attitude. But at this stage, he must be given formal warning by the jail authority. Though punishment should be regarded as a necessary evil and a measure of last resort, yet it should be balanced in relation to the gravity of the violation.[2]

To ensure balanced punishment for violation of prison rules, the West Bengal Jail Code Revision Committee of 1972-73 have recommeded that the Superintendent of a jail who is responsible for safe custody, security and reformation of prisoners should not have unfettered authority to punish prisoners in his custody, and that a *Discipline Committee* be constituted in every jail for enquiring into all offences which might make the superintendent think that infliction of major punishment was desirable. The superintendent is to award such punishment only on the recommendation of the Discipline Committee.[3]

The prison offences are normally divided into two categories : (i) offences which come under the purview of the prison authority, and (ii)offences which come within the purview of the courts. So long as the offence of a prisoner does not cross the first category, the prison authority cannot refer the case to the Magistrate. In *Maqbool Husain V. State of Bombay*,[4] it was held by the Supreme Court that the scheme of Rule 41 of the Punjab Communist Detenus Rules (1950) was to constitute the Jail Superintendent only as the administrative authority to maintain jail discipline and inflict summary punishment on the detenus for breach of that discipline. It was only when the Jail Superintendent considered that the offence was not adequately punishable by him that he could send the case to the Magistrate. If he had himself punished, he could not, under this Rule, refer the case again to the Magistrate. A reference by him after punishment would be wholly unauthorized and the prosecution before the Magistrate would be illegal and not in accordance with procedure established by law.

Various types of punishment, such as death sentence,

transportation for life, simple and rigorous imprisonment fine, etc., are imposed by the courts in accordance with the gravity of the crimes and the provisons of the law. The execution of punishment awarded by the courts, however, lies on the prison authority for which they must realize the nature of the offence and the degree of punishment which the courts or the judges want to be inflicted on the offenders. This is necessary because the execution of punishment imposed by the court is in many cases subject to the discretion which the prison authorities are required, by law of the Jail Code, to apply.

Although crime is as old as society itself, there is no universally accepted definition of crime. The concept of crime, in fact, varies from country to country and from time to time in the same country. The legal conception of crime, however, is inseparably related to punishment. Unless there is a crime and conviction for a crime, there can be no punishment, for a crime is committed when an act prohibited by law and punishable by it is committed.

A crime is not a tort which is a private offence ; it is not merely an offence against the state, but an offence against society as well. Defining crime merely in legal terms, therefore, is not enough. The definition of crime should also include a description of the social nature of the acts prohibited by law. As Sutherland and Cressey have observed : "The statement that we would have no crime if we had no criminal laws and that we could eliminate all crime merely by abolishing all criminal laws is logomachy. It is true that if the laws against stealing were repealed, stealing would not be a crime, but it would still be offensive and the public would react to it by lynch law and public disgrace. The name of the behaviour would be changed but the behaviour and the societal reaction, to the behaviour would remain essentially the same, for the "social interests" damaged by the behaviour would remain essentially unchanged. Because of this, efforts have been made to include within the definition of crime a description of the nature of the acts which the law prohibits and thus to define crime in social rather than legal terms". From the social point of view, crime involves three elements : a value appreciated by a group which is politically powerful ; refusal to recognize this value by persons who do not appreciate it sufficiently or at all, and consequently tend to endanger it; coercion applied decently and in an organized way by the former on the latter. "This conception of the social nature of crime" as Sutherland and Cressey further observe, "is suggestive and may be developed into a fundamental definition, but at present certainly lack precision."[5]

Fixing punishment for a crime also involves cretain problems. Since crime is a threat to, an offence against society, it has got to be prevented. But, the manner in which it is prevented has undergone spontaneous changes with the change of time as well as the progress of human civilization. In the early state of civilization inhuman treatment of offenders was a normal practice. In general terms, it may be said that "with every advance in civilization the punishment and reclamation of the criminal have proceeded on lines which have mitigated force and substituted methods of reformation."[6] The early practice of repression of crimes by blatant application of force is in vogue today in some countries. In Saudi Arabia and Pakistan, for instance, almost inhuman and barbarous punishments as public flogging and mutilation of limbs are inflicted for offences like dacoity, theft and rape in accordance with the *Shariat*. Curiously enough, such barbarity is sought to be justified in the name of *just* punishment. But, who is to determine whether a particular punishment is humane or not, just or unjust, qualitatively or quantitatively ? Is it the society or the organized political community, i.e., the state ? Although public opinion seems to be a great determinant factor, it is desirable that opinions of enlightened judges, penologists and other experts who deal with the crime problem rationally and scientifically should have given proper weightage while resolving such intricate issues as the nature and the quantum of just punishment.

Development of Correctional Philosophy

Modern correctional philosophy has developed through various stages and we have the classical school of penology, the neo-classical school, the Italian school and the modern clinical school.

Cesare Beccaria (1738-94), the first great modern ponologist, inspired the classical school of penology in his widely haralded work, *Crimes and Punishments*, published in 1764. He looked upon punishment as both deterent and preventive, and he believed that punishments should be scaled carefully so that the prospective criminal could calculate that his anticipated gains from the criminal act would be outweighed by the severity of punishment he would receive if apprehenced. No greater punishment than necessary to achieve this end could be justified. But he thought that punishment for a crime must be the same for all individuals, regardless of age, mentality, social status or other conditions. As a true representative of Enlightenment, Beccaria wished to place punishment on a rational and objective basis so that cruel and inequitable penalties for crime and capricious use of judicial authority for the same could be prevented. The English utilitarian philosophers led by Jeremy Bentham (1784-1832) effectively argued in the same way. In France the revolutionary penal code of 1791 attempted to apply the classical theory, and Beccari's principle of "equal punishment for the same crime" was its basis. Although the classical school is now outmoded in certain respects, it has indubitably brought in some improvements in our ideas regarding administration of criminal justice.

The neo-classical school, which emerged during the French Revolution and the period immediately following, primarily made an attempt to cope with some of the difficulties experienced in the application of classical theory. Particularly, the judge was given some discretion in sentencing so that he might take into certain "mitigating circumstances." In consideration of such circumstances, for instance, children and lunatics who are unable to calculate pleasure and pains cannot be regarded as criminals or be punished. The revised French Code of 1819 reflects this individual approach to the criminal.

The Italian or the positive school was led by Ceasare Lombroso (1836-1909), Enrico Ferri (1856-1928) and Raffaele Garofalo (1852-1934), who are often considered the founders of modern criminology. This school held that the "born criminal" was an atavistic throwback to a more primitive stage of human evolution, and that he could be identified by certain definite physical "stigmata," such as asymmetrical cranium, long lower jaw, flattened nose, scanty beard, low sensitivity to pain, and characteristic hair growth on the body (though both Ferri and Garofalo placed an increased emphasis upon social and psychological factors).

Although the Italian school overstated the case for biological factor in criminal etiology and its experimental methodology was faulty in the sense that it failed to compare criminals with non-criminals, it has been of paramount importance in the development of penology, especially for its focus upon the criminal as an individual (rather than upon abstract law or justice), its emphasis on science and scientific method, and its formulation of the social protection theory of punishment.

The modern clinical school accepted the social protection theory of punishment. It has drawn heavily upon auxiliary sciences to achieve its purpose of protecting society by rehabilitating the criminal. New development in psychology, psychiatry, physiology and sociology have been of special value in understanding the causes of crime and criminality and the best methods of dealing with the criminal and his deviant behaviour. John Lewis Gillin (1871-1958), an eminent American criminologist, has described the position of the modern clinical school as follows : "The criminal is the product of his biological inheritence conditioned in his development by the experiences of life to which he has been exposed from early infancy up to the commission of the crime . . . By studying the offender in every possible way, the Modern school promises to throw light on his conditioning and arrive at a diagnosis of the factors entering into each individual case. From the standpoint of penology, this school attempts to adapt the treatment of each individual in accordance with the diagnosis obtained by scientific study of the criminal". In line with this new approach, the term 'correction' is often used today instead of 'penology', indicating that the chief concern is to correct anti-social behaviour, not to punish it.

Various strategies and techniques have been evolved since the later decades of the 19th century in the refinement of the new approach to crime and criminals. Devices such as probation, parole, the indeterminate sentence, individualized treatment of prisoners, and experiments in group living have come to find a place in the modern clinical school of thought. At one time offenders were committed to prison for further punishment ; now they are committed as ultimate punishment. The prisoner is punished by his loss of liberty necessiated by incarceration ; he is sent to prison to receive no additional punishment but a course of correction wherefrom he is expected to regain his former moral self.[7]

The problems of defining a crime and fixing its punishment are not the concern of the prison authority but of the legislature. As the development of penology rests on both the definition of crimes and the nature of punishments, it is also the concern of the legislature and its expert committee. But, for the purpose of administering the law in its true spirit, it is necessary for prison administrators to be acquainted not only with the law but with its purpose as well.

Punishment, excessively heavy or light, defeats its purpose. Enlightened public opinion dislikes excessive punishment. Severe whipping and other very painful punishments ultimately dull fear and stunt sensitiveness in the victim. This is why progressive penologists and jurists throughout the world today are opposed to any kind of harsh punishments and advocate more humane and sympathetic treatment of offenders.

Infliction of punishment is considered to be a part of justice itself, and justice gives each man his due. Neither favour nor frown is to influence the administration of justice either by the judiciary or by the prison authorities. This does not imply that the prison administrators are not to be nourished by the milk of human kindness. To be sure, the slogan of humanitarianism cannot be allowed to defeat the ends of social life, that is, peace, prosperity and happiness for all. But, as Dr. B.K. Bhattacharya observes : "When any punishment is to be inflicted, it should be just sufficient to meet the case and no more."[8]

Theories of Punishment

It may be useful for our present study to review the principal ohjects of punishment. These are commonly held to be (1) retribution or retaliation, (2) expiation, (3) deterrence, (4) reformation, and (5) the protection of society.

The theory of retribution rests on the idea that wrong-doing must on moral principle be followed by adequate physical suffering, irrespective of whether it is imposed by the society or by the victim. 'Eye for an eye and tooth for a tooth' is a barbarous principle and has been attacked on the ground that it equates suffering and wrong-doing not rationally b.t vindictively. Yet, this theory has not died out altogether from the minds of the makers of penal codes even in the present century.

The theory of expiation has a religious touch and rests on the belief that wrong-doing should be atoned by a punishment which can purge the guilty mind of the criminal. In penology the term 'expiation' does not merely imply spiritual repentance but also an endeavour to objectively balance the degree of severity of the crime by that of punishment. Thus, King Henry II of England submitted his naked body to be scourged by his monks as a mark of his repentance over the death of Archbishop Thomas Beckett which was caused by his angry words. Even though there may be no predictable advantage to society from such atonement, it is considered by many as morally necessary.

The theory of deterrence is more objective and rests on the principle that the infliction of punishment or pain upon convicted criminals serves to frighten and thereby to deter other mortals from committing similar acts. This theory was based on the hedonistic assumption of the utilitarians of the 19th century that people regulate their behaviour by calculation of pleasure and pain. It also rests on the belief that the rational criminal is not apt to risk a major penalty for a minor advantage. Modern psychological investigation of deviant behaviour, however, reveals that criminals often act under the stress of momentary passion or emotion and that this impulse is likely to be little controlled by such rational calculations of pleasure and pain.

The theory that the essential purpose of punishment is to bring about moral reformation of the wrong-doer has its roots deep in the Judaic—Christian tradition. True expiation requires, on this theory, some kind of inner or spiritual transformation and not simply a harsh punishment. This concept, old as it is, had little effect on the treatment of criminals until early modern times when the American Quakers and other reformers seriously tried to initiate humanitarian changes.

The theory that the basic purpose of punisment is to protect society has been a supplementary aim of other theories, at least in some of their forms. However, it is the principal justification in contemporary penological systems. Not only does society incarcerate criminals to prevent them from continuing their anti-social acts, but it further protects itself by reeducating and rehabilitating the offender.[9]

So long as the theories of retribution, expiation, and deterrence dominated the penal philosophy, criminal acts were sought to be prevented primarily through infliction of barbarous punishments and there was little or no use of the period of imprisonment for the correction of the prisoner. The principal object of prison administration during the predominance of the earlier theories was to detain the offenders awaiting trial or make them suffer physically. The ascendancy of the theory of reformation is due largely to the humanitarian zeal of the revolutionary penal reformers of the late 18th and early 19th centuries, Unfortunately, these reformers were not free altogether from the influence of the earlier theories of punishment and hence, while recommending the reformation of criminals primarily "through the discipline of punishment," they did not eliminate punishment that was "bone-breaking and brutal", and sometimes even more severe than the earlier days. With the advent of the present century the progressive thinkers of the world began to realize that cruel punishments could not ensure real discipline or achieve reformation. They are insisting for the first time that imprisonment itself is sufficient punishment and that any addition to it will be utterly unjustified. It is at this stage that the social protection theory of punishment gets prominence and consequently the ultimate object of prison administration has, in general terms, undergone a radical change : from reformation through repressive measures to reeducation and rehabilitation of offenders through individualized training and treatment.

Punishments Under West Bengal Jail Code

Punishments for prison offences as laid down under Rule 708 of the Jail Code of West Bengal are divided into two categories : (i) minor punishments, and (ii) major punishments.

The following punishments fall within the category of minor punishments :

1. Formal warning ;
2. Change of labour to some more irksome or severe form for a period not exceeding one month ;
3. Forfeiture of remission earned, not exceeding 4 days ;
4. Forfeiture of prison privileges admissible under the remission system, for a period not exceeding three months ;
5. Separate confinement for not more than 14 days ;
6. Imposition of handcuffs otherwise than by handcuffing a prisoner behind his back ; and
7. Imposition of link fetters for not more than 15 days.

The following punishments are considered to be major punishments :

1. Hard labour, in the case of prisoners not sentenced to rigorous imprisonment ;

1A. Change of labour to some more irksome or severe form for a period exceeding one month ;

2. (a) Forfeiture of remission earned, exceeding 4 but not exceeding 12 days ;
   (b) Forfeiture of remission earned, in excess of 12 days ;
   (c) Forfeiture of prison privileges admissible under the remission system for a period exceeding three months ;
   (d) Exclusion from the remission system for a period not exceeding three months ;
   (e) Exclusion from the remission system for a period exceeding three months ;

3. Separate confinement for a period exceeding 14 days ;
4. Link fetters, if imposed for more than 15 days ;
5. Bar fetters ;
6. Handcuffing behind ; and
7. Any combination of minor punishments admissible under Section 47 of Act IX of 1894.

All the punishments, mentioned above, may be awarded by the Jail Superintendent himself save the major punishments 2(b) and 2(e) and any combination of the major punishments 2(b), 2(c) and 2(e) for which the previous sanction of Inspector-General is required. Under Rule 708A, no officer subordinate to the Superintendent has the power to punish a prisoner except in case of *urgent necessity* where a Jailor may place a prisoner under mechanical restraint.[10] However, the exercise of such drastic power, in the light of historic judgement of the Supreme Court in *Batra's case*,[11] is subject to two basic considerations : (i) security of the prison, and (ii) safety of the prisoners. These and similar considerations bear direct nexus with the safe custody of prisoners as they are aimed primarily at preventing their escapes. The determination of the necessity to put a prisoner in bar fetters (or under any mechanical restraint) has to be made after application of mind to the peculiar and special characteristics of each individual prisoner. Needless to say, the principle of *fairness*[12] demands that the grounds of fetters shall be given to the victim. And when the decision to fetter is made, the reason has to be recorded in the journal and on the prisoner's history ticket in the state language. If he is a stranger to that language it shall be communicated to him, as far as possible, in his lanuage. This applies to cases as much of prison punishment as of safety fetters.[13] The other key jurisdictional pre-conditions laid down by the Supreme Court are :

(i) before preventive or punitive irons (both are inflictions of bodily pain) natural justice[14] in its minimal form shall be complied with (both *audi alteram* implying that no man shall be condemned unheared, and the *nemo judex in re sua* implying that no man shall be judge in his own case) ;

(ii) the fetters shall be removed at the earliest opportunity. That is to say, even if some risk has to be taken it shall be removed unless compulsive considerations continue it for necessities of safety ;

(iii) there shall be a daily review of the absolute need for the fetters, none being easily conceivable for nocturnal manacles ;

(iv) if it is found that the fetters must continue beyond a day, it shall be held illegal unless an outside agency like the District Magistrate or Session Judge, on materials placed, directs its continuance.[15]

These requirements, according to the Court, are reasonably practical and reconcile security with humanity. Moreover, having regard to the penumbral zone, fraught with potential for tension, tantrums and illicit violence and malpractice, the Court suggests very rightly that a *prison ombudsman* should be organized for each State.[16] The ombudsman, *inter alia,* as suggested on the basis of the American judicial practice, is to be responsible for hearing inmate complaints and grievances, conducting investigation and making recommendations to the Court.[17]

Rule 709 lays down that every infringement of jail rules has to be brought to the notice of the Superintendent who shall decide whether the infringement was committed in such circumstances, e.g., wilfully or without excuse, as to constitute an offence. If the Superintendent is of the opinion that the infringement was committed through ignorance or excusable carelessness, he is to admonish the prisoner and dismiss the charge without recording it in the Punishment Register. But, if after communicating to the prisoner concerned the facts alleged against him and giving him an opportunity to state his defence, the Superintendent finds it to be an offence, he has to award some punishment and get it recorded in the Punishment Register and likewise on the prisoner's history ticket.

A 'formal warning,' deemed to be a punishment under Rule 710, may be personally addressed to the offender by the Superintendent. Being ordinarily the punishment for a first offence, it is not combined with any other punishment.

Rules 711 and 732 provide for the punishment of change of labour. Prisoners undergoing rigorous imprisonment are given this punishment, i.e., change of labour to some more irksome or severe form, when guilty of persistent short work, idleness, or other offences. Prisoners sentenced to simple imprisonment may be awarded this punishment in the form of hard labour only when the Medical Officer certifies that they are fit for it. The latter may advice if any modification of this punishment is necessary in view of the prisoner's health. Again, in view of the Supreme Court's judgement in *Batra's case*,[18] a prison official under these Rules cannot force a prisoner to do *harsh* and *degrading* labour. "Punishments of rigorous imprisonment," observed the Court, "oblige the inmates to do hard labour, not harsh labour and so a vindictive officer victimizing a prisoner by forcing on him particularly harsh and degrading jobs, violates the law's mandate. For example, a prisoner, if forced to carry night soil, may seek a habeas writ. 'Hard Labour' in Section 53 (of the Prisons Act of 1894) has to receive a humane meaning. A girl student or a male weakling sentenced to rigorous imprisonment may not be forced to break stones for nine hours a day. The prisoner cannot demand soft jobs but may reasonably be assigned congenial jobs. Sense and sympathy are not enemies of penal asylums."

The Jail Code of West Bengal has imposed certain restrictions on the use of handcuffs and fetters as punishments for prison offences.[19] Rule 717, for instance, lays down that handcuffs may be imposed ; (a) on the wrists in front, by day or night, for a period not more than 12 hours at a time, with intervals of not less than 12 hours and for not more than four consecutive days or nights ; (b) on the wrists behind, by day only, for a period of not more than six hours in any day of twenty-four hours, and for not more than four consecutive days. Moreover, a prisoner undergoing punishment in handcuffs must be under complete shelters from the sun. Rule 719 stipulates that the maximnm period for which fetters may be continuously imposed is to be thirty days. Rule 720 requires an interval of at least ten days between two impositions whether for the same or different offences. Again, under

Rule 730 female, juvenile or civil prisoners are debarred from any handcuffing or imposition of fetters unless there is a likelihood of the woman seriously injuring herself or others, and even then such handcuffiing is not to be for more than 48 hours at a time.

There are regulatory provisions for the imposition of separate confinement as well. Rule 724 stipulates that 'separate confinement' is confinement in a cell, with or without labour, so as to seclude the prisoner whilst in his cell from communication with, but not from sight of, other prisoners. The outer batten door of the cell yard in cells built on the standard plan shall be left open, and a prisoner undergoing this punishment shall have not less than one hour's exercise daily in the common passage in front of the cells or other sufficient space under the eye of a warder, and shall have his meals in association with one or more other prisoners. A jail superintendent may award this punishment up to 30 days, and if any period in excess of this up to 3 months is deemed necessary, the order of the Inspector-General has to be obtained. Moreover, while submitting an application for such order, the Superintendent is required to forward a certificate of the Medical Officer of the prisoner's fitness to undergo separate confinement for the period recommended, or for any other period the Medical Officer may consider the prisoner to undergo.

There is hardly any doubt that in West Bengal prison punishments have been humanized and rationalized to a considerable extent through the revision of law. The Prisons (West Bengal Amendment) Act of 1957 abolished whipping as well as penal diet and wearing of gunny clothing as forms of punishment for prison offences. But unfortunately our prisons still bear the relics of the past. The statutory restrictions on the imposition of irons and separate confinement are observed more in breach than in compliance. It has been alleged that over-zealous prison administrators often impose such inhuman and degrading punishments recklessly and arbitrarily. The report of the world human rights body, Amnesty International, on political prisoners in West Bengal came out in late 1974 with a very serious allegation that several

Naxalite prisoners were being kept in leg irons day and night for more than two years.[20] Obviously, both the Central and the West Bengal State Governments readily reacted to the Amnesty Report in usual apathetic manner of merely denying such allegation without any independent or impartial inquiry. But the fact remains that reckless use of handcuffs and fetters are now common in most of the prisons in our country. As the Supreme Court observed in *Batra's case*,[21] "There is little doubt that barbarities like bar fetters and handcuffs are recklessly being practised either on account of ignorant un conscionableness or wilful viciousness in several detention camps. Many of the victims are poor, mute, illiterate, des perate and destitute and too distant from the law to be aware of their rights or ask for access to justice, especially when the running tension of the prison and the grisly potential for zoological reprisals stare them in the face. So it is for the court to harken when humanity calls, without waiting for particular petitions. Like class actions, class remedies have *pro bono* value."

Separate confinement as a mode of prison punishment has been opposed by many conscientious penologists, jurists and political thinkers in our country and abroad on the ground that it is disastrous to the physical and mental health of the confined. Our Supreme Court too held firmly in *Batra's case*[22] that solitary confinement, cellular segregation and marginally modified editions of the same process (such as separate confinement) were *inhuman* and *irrational.* "More dangerous are these expedients (including irons)", observed the Court, "when imposed by the untuned and untrained power of a jail superior, as part of his professional equipment, no course in human psychology stressology or physiology, who has to depend on med cal or psychiatric examination prior to infliction of irons or solitary, who has no obligation to hear the victim before harming him, whose 'reasons' are in English on the history-tickets and there fore unknowable and in the Journal to which the prisoner has no access. The revisory power of the Inspector General of Prisons is illusory when the prisoner does not know of his right to seek revision and the Inspector General has no duty to visit the solitary or 'fettered creatures' or to examine every case of such infliction... Alternatives to 'solitary' and 'irons' are available to prison technology, given the will, except where indifference, incompetence and unimaginativeness hold prison authorities prisoner. Social justice cannot sleep if the Constitution hangs limp where its consumers most need its humanism".

Thus, the dynamic role of judicial remedies, after *Batra's case*,[23] imparts to the habeas corpus writ a versatile vitality and operational utility that makes the healing presence of the law live up to its reputation as bastion of liberty even within the secrecy of the hidden cell.[24] Consequently, the concept of punishment of offenders has undergone significant changes in the context of the modern *reformist* theory of punishment. "It is no more open to debate", as the Supreme Court observed forthrightly, "that convicts are not wholly denuded of their fundamental rights. However, a prisoner's liberty is in the very nature of things circumscribed by the very fact of his confinement. His interest in the limited liberty left to him is then all the more substantial. Conviction for a crime does not reduce the person into a non-person whose rights are subject to the whim of the prison administration and, therefore, the imposition of any major punishment within the prison system is conditional upon the observance of procedural safeguards".[25]

Remission of Sentence

The system of granting remission or reduction of sentence has been an integral part of our prison administration for over a century now.[26] Although this system has been criticized by some penologists as a sort of bribe for good behaviour, it is fairly well established now that the system, if adequately applied, will act as an effective instrument for encouraging habits of industry and promoting good conduct among prisoners. "Hope of remission or reduction of the period of sentence", observes Dr. Bhattacharya very poignantly, "is agreat sustaining factor. With his mind fixed on earning a remission a prisoner will try to improve himself, and the fear of losing the remission will deter him from mischief. 'Chronophobia' or fear of time may be alleviated to a certain extent. It may be the one bright ray in a world of settled, hopeless expectation of utter misery".[27]

At present the system of granting remission to inmates varies from State to State and there is no uniform mechanism for the grant of remission on a rational or objective basis. As the All India Committee on Jail Reforms (1980-83) observed: "Although the Model Prison Manual containing *inter-alia* guidelines in this respect was circulated to all States and Union Territories as long back as in 1960, there has not been any uniformity in the grant of remissions in the country. There is also a widespread feeling that remission system is generally operated upon in an arbitrary manner with little or no regard to the individual differences and merits of the case. There have been complaints by the prisoners about the manner and mode of granting remission in several places. It is alleged that the grant of remission is guided by the whims and fancies of the persons competent to grant it, and as such crafty prisoners manoeuvre the system to their advantage. The grant of remission constitutes an area highly prone to corrupt practices if the discretion in this regard is not exercised judiciously".[28]

Generally speaking, there are now four types of remission of sentences : (i) ordinary remission ; (ii) annual good conduct remission ; (iii) special remission ; and (iv) State remission. Each type differs from the others in respect of the criteria for eligibility, procedure for award and the authority competent to grant it.[29]

Under the Jail Code of West Bengal,[30] three kinds of remission may be awarded to the prisoner, viz., ordinary, special and State. Ordinary remission is awarded at the rate of two days per month for thoroughly good conduct and scrupulous attention to all prison regulations, and two days per month for industry and the due performance of the daily task imposed. In addition, one day's ordinary remission per month may be awarded to the prisoners employed in prison services, such as cooks and sweepers, who work on Sundays and holidays. Special remission is given for special services such as success in teaching handicrafts to others, protecting a prison-officer from attack, proficiency as a teacher or pupil in the Jail School. Special remission is also awarded for blood donation. State remission is granted by the State Government on the occasion of public rejoicing, e.g., in connection with Independence Day, Republic Day, etc.

The remission system prescribed by the Jail Code of West Bengal seems to be 'mechanical' and requires certain modifications in the light of the latest trends in penology. As suggested by the All India Jail Manual Committee of 1957-59, special remission should be granted only on a selective basis.[31] The West Bengal Jail Code Revision Committee (1972-73)[32] recommended the following measures for evolving an effective system of special remission :

1. A Committee under the nomenclature of 'Remission Committee' should be constituted. The proposed Discipline Committee may also function as the Remission Committee. This Committee will examine all cases of special remission and recommend to the Superintendent what special remission should be granted to individual prisoners.
2. The existing rule of granting special remission for donation of blood should be changed as it has given rise to many practical difficulties and complications. Prisoners donating blood should be paid in cash at the rate fixed by Government Blood Banks.

Some prison admistrators are of the opinion that habitual offenders should not be granted any concession of remission. The All India Jail Manual Committee (1957-59)[33], however, very reasonably held that habitual offenders should not be totally debarred from the benefit of remission, but their eligibility should be thoroughly scrutinized on the basis of their efforts for self-improvement. The All India Committee on Jail Reforms (1980-83)[34] also felt that the system of remission as an instrument of effecting change in the attitude of inmates towards work and behaviour should be liberalized and its ambit enlarged so as to encompass more categories of inmates within its scope. It suggested *inter alia* the following scale of remission for habitual prisoners :

(i) 2 days per calendar month for good behaviour, discipline and participation in institutional activities ;

(ii) 2 days per calendar month for due performance of work according to prescribed standards ;

(iii) 5 days per calendar month for prisoners who are night watchman, or are engaged on conservancy work, or as cooks, or on prison maintenance services requiring them to work even on Sundays and holidays.

Conclusion

The enforcement of ordinary rules of discipline in a prison is a difficult task. Since punishment is a measure of last resort for the enforcement of prison discipline it should be balanced in relation to the gravity of the violation of rules. Some kind of mechanism has also to be evolved to restrain abuse of power by the overzealous prison officials, and to that end, the recommendations of the Supreme Court and some of the official committees, as discussed in this chapter, are of great value.

The convenventional approach to prison discipline and punishment need to be changed. With the development of modern criminal school of thought and the ascendancy of the social protection theory of punishment the basic purpose of prison administration has undergone a radical change. The prisoner is now committed to prison to receive no additional punishment but a course of correction necessary for his moral regeneration and ultimate resettlement in the mainstream of social life. If these new thoughts are to find any meaningful expression in the Indian jail system, there is no alternative to the will to change.

Since remission of prison sentence is a great sustaining factor "in a world of settled, hopeless expectation of utter misery", the existing system of granting remission has to be overhauled in such a manner that it may operate objectively as a positive incentive to prisoners for good behaviour and work rather than as a 'mechanical' system guided by the "whims and fancies" of the prison officials and "manoeuvred" by the crafty prisoners to their advantage.

NOTES AND REFERENCES

1. Government of India, *Model Prison Manual*, 1960, p. 194.
2. Government of India. *Report of the All India Jail Manual Committ* (1957-59), Para 106 and *Model Prison Manual*, p. 194.
3. *Report*, [.p. 67. The Discipline Committee, according to 'Mod Prison Manual', is to be constituted with Supterintendent Chairman and Deputy Suptd. and Senior Asstt. Suptd. as member:
4. AIR 1953, S.C. 325 (332) ; 1953 Cri. L.J. 1432.
5. Edwin H. Sutherland and Donald R. Cressey, *Principles of Crimin logy*, 2nd Indian Reports Reprint, 1968, pp. 14-15.
6. Govt. of West Bengal, *Report of the West Bengal Jail Code Revisi Committee* (1972-73), p. 3.
7. The material for discussion on the thoughts of different schools penology is drawn from *Encyclopedia Americana*, Edn. 1966, Vol. 2 pp. 541-42 ; David Dressler, *Practice and Theory of Probation a People*, 2nd edn., 2nd Printing, 1971, pp. 5-15.
8. B.K. Bhattacharya, *Prisons*, 1958. p. 116.
9. The material for discussion on the theories of punishment is dra from *Encyclopedia Americana, op. cit.* pp. 540-41 ; N.C. Pal, *Crim Cause and Cure*, 1963, pp. 37-38.
10. In such a case the Jailor has to bring the matter to the Superinte dent's notice with lhe least possible delay (Rules 708 B).
11. *Sunil Batra v. Delhi Administration*, AIR 1978 SC 1675 at 1678.
12. *Maneka Gandhi v. Union of India*, AIR 1978, S.C. 597.
13. *Supra* note 11 at 1724.
14. For details see S.S. Singh, *Administration of Natural Justice in Ind* 1986.
15. *Supra* note 11 at 1719.
16. *Supra* note 11 at 1720.
17. *Sunil Batra v. Delhi Administration*, AIR 1980 S.C. 1579 at 1599.
18. *Ibid.* at 1594.
19. Even these restrictions are now required to be modified in the li of the Supreme Court's judgement in *Batra's case* as discussed earl in this Chapter.
20. For further details on Amnesty International Report see Anan Rahula, "Prisoners of Conscience," *Illustrated Weekly*, March 1975.
21. *Supra* note 17 at 1951-92 per Krishna Iyer, J.
22. *Supra* note 11 at 1720 per Krishna Iyer, J.
23. (1979) 1 SCR 392 : AIR 1978 SC 1675.
24. *Supra* note 17 at 1582 per Krishna Iyer, J.

25. *Supra* note 11.
26. Govt. of India : Ministry of Home Affairs, *Report of All India Committee on Jail Reforms* (1980-83), Vol. I, p. 238.
27. B.K. Bhattacharya, *op. cit.*, p. 109.
28. Vol. I, p. 238 of the Committee's Report.
29. *Ibid.*
30. Chapter XXI.
31. Para 100 of the Committee's Report.
32. pp. 65 and 67 of the Committee's Report.
33. Para 100 of the Committee's Report.
34. Vol. I, pp. 239-40 of the Committee's Report.

8

CAPITAL PUNISHMENT AND SOCIAL REHABILITATION OF PRISONERS

In this chapter are discussed two subjects which, though diametrically opposed to each other, are now being seriously considered by penal reformers all over the world. Their inclusion in the same chapter highlights the contrast that is involved in the minds of those who conceive them as necessary. Society has long been using capital punisment as a last resort to combat the gravest of crimes which threaten its foundation as well as its moral code. According to the British Royal Commission on Capital Punishment (1949-53), of the three commonly known principal purposes of punishment-retribution, deterrence and reformation-deterrence has occupied the greatest attention in the assessment of the importance of capital punishment. The general conclusion which the Commission has reached, after careful review of all the evidence at their disposal as to the deterrent effect of capital punishment, is that : "*prima facie* the penalty of death is likely to have a stronger effect as a deterrent to normal human beings than any other form of punishment, and there is some evidence (though no convincing statistical evidence) that this is in fact so. But this effect does not operate universally or uniformly, and there are many offenders on whom it is limited and may often be negligible. It is accordingly important to view this question in a just perspective and not to base a penal policy in relation to murder on exaggerated estimates of the uniquely deterrent force of the death penalty".[1]

Although human civilization has traversed "a long way from the horrors of Newgate where men were strung up for picking pockets", the long debate on the efficacy of capital punishment as a deterrent has not yet been resolved. Some countries have abolished the death sentence while others are in favour of retaining it. And there are others where the penalty exists as a law, but is rarely enforced.

In the United States the death penalty has been abolished without any reservation only in some states, viz., Minnesota, Wiscansin, Dltware etc. A few others have abolished it with some qualifications. For instance, Michigan has retained it for treason only; North Dakota, treason or murder by a lifer and Rhode Island, murder by a lifer.[2] In *Furman V. Georgia*[3] US Supreme Court observed : "Death penalty should be outlawed on the grounds that it is an anachronism, degrading to human dignity and unnecessary in modern life". In England there was a long debate on the issue following the recommendation of the Royal Commission on Capital Punishment (1949-53) for its abolition. The debate came to an end with the abolition of death sentence in that country in 1965. In recent times, France and the German Democratic Republic also abolished death penalty.

The Israelis have the "unenviable" record of being one of the most persecuted nations of the world. Tne barbaric crimes perpetrated on them during the World War II by the Nazis have left in them a persecution complex and a thirst for vengeance. But, as Dr. Hiranandani says, they have also "abolished the death penalty in their own country — the only exception being the hanging of Eichman (killer of over half a million Jews during the War)."[4]

In most of the Islamic States, viz. Sa'udi Arabia, Iran and Pakistan, where the penal system is based on the dictums of the *Shariyat*, not only has the death penalty been retained but cruel and barbaric modes of execution such as stoning to death also exist. Public hanging has been the common practice not only in these countries but also in some Socialist States such as China.

For many years there has been a great movement on the part of thousands of enlightened and humane thinkers, social refomers and jurists for the abolition of capital punishment on the ground that it is barbarous, inhuman and degrading. Mahatma Gandhi, a staunch abolitionist, viewed this punishment as a negation of *ahimsa* or non-violence. As he once wrote in the *Harijan* : "God alone can take life because He alone gives it.... Destruction of individuals can never be a virtuous act. The evil-doers cannot be done to death". Describing capital punishment as "a barbaric practice", his distinguished disciple Jayaprakash Narayan said, "punishment for crime should be aimed at reformation of the criminal and not his extermination. We have no right to take life when we cannot give life."

Many great thinkers of the West have expressed similar views. To quote the words of Victor Husgo : "We shall look upon cirme as a disease. Evil will be treated in charity instead of anger. The change will be simple and sublime. The Cross shall displace the scaffold. Reason is on our side, feeling is on our side, and experience is on our side". Dostoevsky once said that if, in the last moment before being executed, a man, however brave,was givan the alternative of spending the rest of his numbered days on the top of a bare rock, with only enough space to sit on it, he would choose it with relief. "The gallows", as Arthur Koestler puts it, "is not only a machine of death but a symbol. It is the symbol of terror, cruelty and irreverence for life ; the common denominator of primitive savagery, medieval fanaticism and modern totalitarianism. It stands for everything that mankind must reject, if mankind is to survive its present crisis."[5] The declaration adopted by the Internatioal Canference on the Abolition of Death Penalty, convened by Amnesty International at Stockholm in December, 1977, says : "Capital Punishment is the ultimate, cruel, inhuman and degrading punishment and violates the right to life—the basic right of man. It ought to be abolished in all its forms."

Ironically, this inhuman, brutal and degrading type of punishment is still retained in the land of Buddha and Gandhi. Indian public sentiment has not yet been aroused against its retention despite a prolonged movement for its abolition by Jayaprakash Narayan, J.B. Kripalani and other distinguished Gandhians. Way back in 1956 the Central Government invited opinions from the States on this issue. The verdict was in favour of retention. In 1967, the Law Commission recommended its retention in view of the paramount need to maintain law and order. The situation today does not show even the slightest sign of improvement. On the contrary, there is enough evidence of an increase in atrocities on Harijans and in mass killings, rape and maiming by gangsters and in organized violence and terrorist activities in different parts of the country which could easily make the suffering millions clamour for a more stringent application of the death penalty.[6]

Official statistics, however, reveal that in practice both the sentence and execution of the death penalty are restricted and this is so because our judges and authorities are still guided by "the evolving standards of decency of a maturing society". Against 18,649 cases of murder in 1974 and 17,563 in 1975, only 163 and 96 persons respectively were sentenced to death. Of them only 65 and 26 were executed after their mercy petitions were rejected by the President.

Since the abolition of capital punishment involves serious issues such as law and order, justice and social security, we should be guided by reason and practical considerations instead of emotion, sentiment or religious feeling. A compromise between retention and abolition seems to be most desirable in the context of the present state of public order and security in India. To this end, we may readily accept the enlightened view of Justice Chandrachud. To quote his words : "Capital punishment should not be wiped out from the statute-book, but a judge's first concern should be to avoid imposing the death sentence except in the rarest of cases. Deterrence is not the only object of punishment. There are cases of uncommon brutality in which a judge with a conscience cannot feel that justice is done unless the offender is visited with the highest penalty permissible under the law. It is like cases in which the grossness of defamation deserves the highest award of compensation commensurate with the measure of reputation."[7]

Whether death penalty is abolished or not, it is generally agreed that our existing laws for the award of capital punishment require certain modifications though it is difficult to state them in specific terms. Some have suggested that "it would be a good idea to have psychiatrists and social workers to advice our judges before death sentence is awarded. This could pave the way for a more humane attitude towards the wretched in our society."[8] But the difficulty is just to know whether these advisers would be as independent and impartial in their decision as the judge.

Constitutional Validity of Capital Punishment

Indian judiciary views capital punishment as having been recognized by our constitution. In *Jagmohan Singh v. U.P.*,[9] the appellant, who had been sentenced to death for murder, appealed against his sentence on the ground that the sentence of death violated Article 19. Although this Article did not directly deal with the freedom to live, such freedom was inferred, as the seven freedoms conferred by Article 19(1) could not exist or be real without it. Further, as Article 19 lays down that no one could be deprived of any one of these seven freedoms unreasonably or except in the public interest, it was contended that no one could be deprived of life also without such deprivation being reasonable or in the public interest. In the face of this argument the Supreme Court started with the assumption that the right to live was basic to the freedoms mentioned in Article 19 and that no law could deprive a citizen of his life unless it was reasonable and in the public interest. On this assumption, so was held by the Supreme Court, the question for determination was whether Section 302 of the Indian Penal Code-which prescribed the sentence of death for murder-passed the above test. On this issue the appellant's argument was based on the majority decision of the U.S. Supreme Court in *Furman v. Georgia*, that the sentence of death violated the 8th Amendment to the U.S.

Constitution which prohibited "cruel and unusual punishments." After a careful analysis of the majority and minority judgements in that case and other relevant cases and reports, Justice Palekar observed that the Court had grave doubts about the expediency of transplanting Western experience in our country. Further, our Constitution contained no provision corres ponding to the 8th Amendment to the U.S. Constitution, and the courts were not at liberty to apply the test of reasonableness with the freedom which the Supreme Court of U.S.A. possessed by virtue of the "due process" clause. The framers of the Indian Constitution knew that capital punishment was permissible under the then law. They could have abolished it if they liked. On the contrary, several Articles of the Constitution of India,[10] as finally adopted, expressly refer to and thus recognize capital punishment.

In another landmark case of death penalty, *Bachan Singh v. State of Punjab*,[11] the Supreme Court, in a majorlty judgement, rejected the appellant's challenge to the constitutionality of the death sentence, but at the same time, warning against frequent infliction of this extreme panalty. It observed :

> Judges should never be blood-thirsty. Hanging of murderers has never been too good for them. Facts and figures, albeit incomplete, furnished by the Union of India, in the instant case, show that in the past, Courts have inflicted the extreme penalty with extreme infrequency—a fact which attests to the caution and compassion which they have always brought to bear on the exercise of their sentencing discretion in so grave a matter. It is, therefore, imperative to voice the concern that courts...will discharge the onerous function with evermore scrupulous care and human concern directed along the high road of legislative policy outlined in S. 354(3), viz., that for persons convicted of murder, life imprisonment is the rule and death sentence an exception. A real and abiding concern for the dignity of human life postulates resistance to taking a life through law's instrumentality. That ought not to be done save in the rarest of rare cases when the alternative option is unquestionably foreclosed.

Article 72(1)(c) of the Constitution of India empowers the President of India to grant pardons, reprieves, respites or remission of punishment or to suspend, remit or commute the sentence of any person convicted of any offence in all cases where the sentence is a sentence of death. The following table shows the fate of mercy petitions to the President for the period 1951-79 from persons sentenced to death :

TABLE 9

Fate of Mercy Petitions to the President from Persons Sentenced to Death 1951-79

Period	Total No. of Petitions	Death sentence commuted	Petitions Rejected
1951-56	1,234	342	892
1957-62	1,345	381	962
1963-68	1,003	471	532
1969-74	379	179	200
1975-79	143	46	98

Source : Ministry of Home Affairs, Govt. of India.

As regards the exercise of this power by the President, Dr. L.H. Hiranandani rightly says that "the policy of granting reprieves and pardons must be welcomed, but it must be consistent. Until we apply equal standards to all criminals, it is meaningless to talk of socialism (or justice ?). Remember the beautiful Shamim Rehmani ? She readily got a pardon and is now on her way to stardom and glory instead of leading the life of a discredited citizen or an outcaste. Why shouldn't there be more such cases of reprieve ?"[12] The sentence of Shamim Rehmani was not capital ; but the warning of Dr. Hiranandani applies equally to all cases of reprieve and pardon.

Mode of Execution

Although the Indian courts have been inflicting "the extreme penalty with extreme infrequency," it is still too early to assume that it will be deleted from the statute book in near future. It wil not, therefore, be inappropriate to consider the question whether the mode of execution could be humanized.

In *Janardau Ready V. the State of Hyderabad*[13] seven people accused of murder were sentenced to death by hanging by the Special Tribunal and this was later confirmed by the High Court of Hyderabad, although under Schedule 4 of the Criminal Procedure Code of Hyderabad the death sentence was to be executed by separating the head from the body of the convicted prisoner. In their petitions to the Supreme Court after the commencement of the Constitution, the accused referred to the discrepancy in the mode of execution of the death sentence. Overruling the objection of the petitioners, the Supreme Court observed : "The mode of execution of a sentence can hardly be regarded as a matter of substantive law or something which would affect any substantive rights." If, however, the Cr. P.C. of Hyderabad had prescribed execution of the death sentence by hanging and the Special Tribunal or the High Court had sentenced the accused to death by decapitation, in the humble opinion this writer, it would have been extremely difficult to accept the views of the Supreme Court. For, decapitation would undoubtedly offend our sense of decency and humanism and be regarded as an unusually cruel punishment.[14]

Under the Muslim rule in India, the methods of execution of the death penalty were painful, brutal and inhuman, viz., stoning an offender to death, burying him alive, etc. It has been the practice since the British rule to use hanging as the only method of execution in our country. Before considering the question as to whether our present practice of hanging the offenders sentenced to death would be replaced by a more humane technique, let us have a look into the various alternatives to hanging practised in countries where the death penalty still prevails.

There are four main methods of execution other than hanging used in the western world today. The following table shows the distribution of these methods including hanging :

Electrocution—23 States of the U.S.A.
Guillotine —France.

Hanging	–England, Scotland, British Common-Wealth Countries, 10 States of the U.S.A.
Lethal Gas	—8 States of the U.S.A.
Shooting	—The State of Utah in America allows a choice between hanging and shooting. Shooting is also used in almost all the countries as the mode of exeecution of those sentenced to death for offences against the Military Code.[15]

In terms of the present-day standards of humanism, the methods of execution ought to be certain, simple, quick and decent. The improved method of execution by hanging was considered quick, certain and painless by the Royal Commission on Capital Punishment (1949-53). The noose is now so fitted round the convict's neck that the knot is drawn tight under the left jaw, where it is held in position with a sliding ring. This innovation causes death by "fracture, dislocation of cervical vertebrae with laceration or crushing of the cord." Expert evidence recorded by the Royal Commission was that "any such dislocation causes immediate unconsciousness and there is no chance of a later recovery of consciousness since breathing is no longer possible. The heart may continue to beat for up to twenty minutes, but this is a purely automatic function."[16] This improved method has ensured certainty of death and thereby helps avoid mistakes and double execution. Earlier, even in England where centuries of practice had produced a detailed chart relating a convict's weight and physical condition to the proper length of drop, mistakes had been made. In 1927, a surgeon who witnessed a double execution wrote :

> The bodies were cut down after fifteen minutes and placed in an ante-chamber, when I was horrified to hear one of the supposed corpses give a gasp and find him making respiratory efforts, evidently a prelude to revival. The two bodies were quickly suspended again for a quarter of an hour longer. Dislocation of the neck is the ideal aimed at, but, out of all my post-mortem findings, that has proved

rather an exception, and in the majority of instances the cause of death was strangulation and asphyxia.[17]

The improved method of hanging has another advantage of easing the victim's last agonies of "a slow and distressing death" by suffocation. On the score of simplicity also, hanging has an advantage since the equipment required for it is simpler than that required for either electrocution or execution by lethal gas.

Execution by hanging does not, however, pass the test of "decency." The distortion caused to the body of the victim is bound to produce a grim sight. In some cases the tongue protrudes from the mouth of the 'terror-stricken" convict. Amazingly, even on the verge of death the aesthetic sense does prevail so much in the minds of some convicts that they try their utmost to save their face and features from distortion.

Modern techniques of electrocution, now widely applied for judicial execution in the USA, also ensure speedy and painless death without producing any evil effects like burning or mutilation which are traditionally associated with the electric chair. The leg which comes into direct contact with the electrodes may sometimes be slightly burnt, but the body of the victim is not otherwise marked or mutilated. As we understand from the observation of the Royal Commission of England which inspected the operation of electrocution of some prisons in the USA, the electric chair is "a simple apparatus," the only disadvantage being its dependence on outside commercial sources for the supply of electricity. This disadvantage can hardly be considered a firm ground for its rejection. Indeed, it would not be difficult to receive necessary cooperation from the electric supply agencies, particularly in view of the recent trend towards a reduced number of executions in most countries where the death penalty exists. Surely, these factors are enough to turn the scale in favour of electrocution.[18] The fact that both the English Royal Commission and the Indian Law Commission preferred to retain hanging was not so much for the reason that hanging was considered better than electrocution but for a different reason. As the Royal Commission said : "The scales are weighted in favour of the established practice. If capital punishment were now being introduced in this country for the first time, we do not think it likely that this way of carrying it out (hanging) would be chosen."[19]

There is still another alternative to hanging which has not so far been extensively used but which can be relied on "to inflict death as painlessly and certainly as hanging but with greater decency." This is administration of a lethal drug, a barbiturate such as hexobarbitone or thiopentone by an injection. The effect of the drug on a person is sedative and has also been described as "pleasant," "romantic" and "lovely." As the Royal Commission says, "in about 20 to 30 seconds, perhaps before the dose was completed, the drug would reach the brain. The prisoner would then become unconscious and die a minute or two later. There would be no danger or failure if a large enough dose were given, and the prisoner would feel nothing after the prick of the needle."[20] The preliminaries to this method of execution were also stated to be simple.

The effect of the lethal drug can be duly accomplished if it is applied intravenously. But, as it appears from the Report of the Royal Commission,[21] this operation is beset with at least two difficulties. First, it is never easy to give an intravenous injection to a person unless he is entirely acquiescent. Secondly, it is impossible to give it to anyone having certain physical abnormalities. These conditions are rare but have not yet been proved scientifically superable. Until such progress is achieved in the science of anaesthetics as would enable us to overcome these difficulties with reasonable certainty, we cannot proceed to a point of accepting lethal injection as the only method of execution. Even so there is no reason why a willing convict with a suitable physique should be deprived of choosing his death in a most decent and humane manner.

So we suggest that our existing laws should be amended to provide for three methods of execution : lethal injection, electrocution and hanging ; and let the convict decide for himself in which way he wants to die. If, however, he fails or refuses to make a choice or puts any restraint to the process of execution chosen by him, the choice then should be left to the state.[22]

Social Rehabilitation of Prisoners

The problem of social rehabilitation of prisoners is, with the passing of years, assuming larger dimensions in almost every country of the world. This is so because the moral consciousness of human being which is reluctant to inflict capital punishment even on those who commit gravest crimes, is more actively manifest in the anxiousness of society to secure the redemption and rehabilitation of those who by committing less serious offences, have strayed away for the time being from the normal walks of social life.

For various reasons, juvenile offenders should have received top priority in any programme of social rehabilitation of convicts. The Declaration of Sixth United Nations Congress on Prevention of Crime and Treatment of Offenders, held at Caracas, Venezuela in 1980 recognized that "a high degree of social attention should be paid to the ways in which juveniles are handled, because of their early stage of development."[23]

Although juvenile delinquency is a world-wide problem, there are divergencies in magnitude of the problem consistent with socio-cultural and socio-political differences within and between countries. According to the latest edition of an official report, *Crime in India-1982,* there has been "continuous increase" in the number of juvenile crime during the decade 1973-82. Table 10 shows that from 3.4 per cent in 1973, the proportion of juvenile crime to total cognizable crime has increased to 4.4 per cent in 1982. The volume of juvenile crime per lakh of population has also increased from 6.4 in 1973 to 8.4 in 1982.

Juvenile delinquency is not only a problem for a developing country like ours but for the most advanced country like America as well. "Most crime in the United States," says an official publication,[24] "is committed by the youth. Over 350,000 children or about 30 per cent of all offenders, are under the custody and supervision of juvenile correctional institutions or agencies on any given day."

If these data are of any significance, it is that the problem of juvenile delinquency is stupendous and growing and deserves urgent attention. Since the children of today are citizens of tomorrow, efforts should made to save them from

TABLE 10

Juvenile Delinquency under IPC Crime
(1973-82)

Year	Population in millions (Estimated mid-year)	Total Cognizable Crime cases under IPC	Total Juvenile Crime cases under IPC	% of Juvenile Crime to total Cognizable crime	Volume of Juvenile Crime per lakh of population
1973	573.4	1077181	36469	3.4	6.4
1974	588.3	1192277	40666	3.4	6.9
1975	600.8	1160520	39888	3.4	6.6
1976	613.3	1093897	37015	3.4	6.0
1977	625.8	1267004	44008	3.5	7.0
1978	638.4	1344968	44284	3.3	6.9
1979	651.0	1336168	46351	3.5	7.1
1980	663.6	1368529	55129	4.0	8.3
1981	690.1	1385757	61019	4.4	8.8
1982	705.2	1353904	59345	4.4	8.4

Source.. *Crime in India*, 1974, 1978 and 1982, B.P.R. and D., Ministry of Home Affairs, Govt. of India.

going astray as a part of our investment for the country's future.

Next to juvenile delinquents, the female offenders should receive special attention in social rehabilitation programmes and services in view of the vital role of women in their capacity as mothers in the family. Unfortunately, because of the small number of women offenders throughout the world, they often do not receive adequate attention and consideration and this often results in limited access for women to the necessary programmes and services, including placement in detention facilities, far from their families and home communities. The 'Caracas Declaration', therefore, emphasized the need for deinstitutionalization as an appropriate disposition for women offenders to enable them to discharge their family responsibilities.[25] Deinstitutionalization requires that programmes and services used as alternatives to imprisonment, such as probation, and parole, are made available to female offenders. The rehabilitation of the adult first offenders as well as the recidivists also deserve adequate attention.

The modern philosophy of rehabilitation can be put to practical application only by the development of four related and continuous phases of the correctional process, viz., (i) Probation, (ii) Institutional training and treatment, (iii) Parole, and (iv) After-care service. Since the process of institutional training and treatment has already been discussed in earlier chapters, we shall now deal only with Probation, Parole and After-care service.

Probation

Probation is the major development in correctional techniques over the last two or three decades. It is "a court action which permits the convicted offender to retain his freedom in the community, subject to court control and the supervision and guidance of a probation officer. Probation sustains the offender's ability to continue working and to protect his family's welfare, while avoiding the stigma and possible damaging effects of imprisonment."[26] Probation is, therefore, a non-punitive method of dealing with offenders as well as an acceptable substitute for imprisonment.

The chief aims of probation are : (i) to prevent further development of the criminal propensities in offenders, and (ii) to provide them with an opportunity to return to their natural setting in the free community instead of sending them to "the unnatural and too often socially harmful atmosphere of prisons". It is, however, the rehabilitative element that actually gives meaning to the preventive aspect of probation, and this is . why, rehabilitation may reasonably be regarded as the "soul" of probation.

Probation has considerable advantages both to the person on probation and the community as a whole. From the standpoint of the person on probation, as D.N. Ray points out :

(i) It affords him a chance to rectify his habits and conduct and to readjust himself to the community.
(ii) It sustains his ability to continue working, to meet family obligations, and to participate in any other activities that have meaning to him as a social being.
(iii) It lessens the social stigma of a prison sentence.

From the standpoint of the community, as Shri Ray has mentioned further :

(i) It saves the expense of maintaining the offender in an institution.
(ii) It gets an immediate contribution to the total national income from the offender through his working for himself and his family or a deferred one through a purposeful use of his working time in socially approved pursuits suited to his age.
(iii) The impact of Probation work and of the Probation Officer working on a case on pathological social situations encountered in the processes is both preventive and curative.[27]

It is generally believed that the probation system is effective particularly in cases of juvenile and first offenders. But as a matter of fact, even carefully selected recidivists can effectively be brought under this system. As M.A. Subramaniam has aptly pointed out, "Rehabilitation is the true antidote for recidivism generally and most of the recidivists are anxious to come back to normal life at some stage or other because their very nature and conscience yearns for freedom and recognition. Unless compelled by adverse conditions the majority may not want to revert to crime. Probation takes note of this fundamental trait in human nature and works upon it." However, as Shri Subramaniam points out further, "Probation is not a magic. It is a scientific method of study and treatment with rehabilitation as the goal. Evidently the cooperation of the police, judiciary and the public is essential for this. [28]

Inter-agency cooperation between the police and the probation service is bound to strengthen the probation work. Despite functional and attitudinal dissimilarities the police, with their resources and professional expertise in dealing with offenders, might help the probation officers by giving them necessary information about the conduct, behaviour and the doings of the probationers and keeping the probationers on surveillance, as and when necessary, without harassing them unnecessarily. The police officer should get himself involved in surveillance only when he will be requested by the probation officer to do so. The probation officer, on the other hand, should avoid taking police help for surveillance unless it is extremely necessary. He should also ensure that the probationers under him are not harassed by the police. All these will be possible only when the two departments function in close liaison with each other, and for this, regular meetings of the officers of these two services will be of great help. "Both the departments", says an expert in this field,[29] "should be actively represented on all organizations relating to corrections including private agencies. In consultation with the probation officer, minor infractions by the probationer could best be condoned by the police with a firm warning". There is also the need to impart special police training in probation work on a selective basis.

Inter-agency cooperation between the police and the judiciary is also of utmost importance for dealing with probation cases more effectively. The application of the law of probation requires the exercise of a sound judicial discretion.

As one legal expert aptly observes, "Justice would be undermined and respect for constituted authority would become a mockery if hardened criminals escaped with undserved probation. But the exercise of such discretion by judges would very much depend upon the thoroughness and care with which the pre-trial investigations were carried out. The task of the judge who had to pass the final order is by no means easy. He had to keep in view conflicting interests and then arrive at a decision which should satisfy all standards with which his decision must be judged. The court should, therefore, have the confidence that the materials placed before them (by the police) was such as would aid them in arriving at their conclusions as to what was best, both for the society and the individual offender".[30]

There is also the need for a change in judicial approach to probation. As the report of the West Bengal Code Revision Committee (1972-73) observes :

> In order to promote and strengthen probation work the first suggestion is to get the judiciary involved in the correctional system, which probation connotes. It is not enough to pass a law and say that probation is a good thing, but the judiciary and the Bar have to be convinced of its advantages and become its votaries.[31]

Finally, public participation and cooperation are considered to be the hall-mark of successful probation work. Members of public as representatives of a community can considerably help in application and promotion of probation not only through their "understanding, support and sympathy" but also by taking active part as voluntary social workers. Voluntary agencies can contribute significantly to promote and strengthen the probation work by setting up Societies and Homes for the rehabilitation of probation cases. The members of these organizations may also work as Voluntary Probation Officers. Under Section 13(1)(b) of the Probation of Offenders Act 1958, a person provided for the purpose by a 'Society' recognized in this behalf by the state government can be appointed as Probation Officer. Unfortunately, most of the state governments have not so far evinced much interest to utilize the services of voluntary probation officers. As the Mulla Committee have very poignantly observed : "The Indian probation system is seriously handicapped for want of adequate number of departmentally paid probation officers and this deficiency ean be effectively remedied by utilizing the services of voluntary workers".[32] Voluntary Women organization will be particularly helpful and effective in dealing with female and juvenile probation cases.

Parole

Parole is a form of conditional release granted to the prisoners after they have served a portion of their sentences. The conditional release involves a service which includes the control, assistance, and guidance the offenders need as they serve the remainder of their sentences within the free community.

Parole is related to but differs from probation. Like probation, parole also ideally includes treatment in the form of supervision, guidance, and assistance. But while in the case of probation the suspension of sentence is made at the court level without the offender having served any part of the sentence in penal confinement, parole is granted by an executive board or the institution itself only after a prisoner has served a portion of his sentence.

Parole is advantageous both for the person released on parole and the society as a whole. Almost all contemporary penologists agree that if a prisoner is to be released at all he should be released on parole. It is rightly held that all released prisoners can benefit from the guidance of parole officers, but the benefit that society itself would derive if all prisoners were kept under close surveillance during the period of adjustment immediately following incarceration, is also considerable.[33]

Despite these advantages, certain precautions need to be taken in the application of parole so as to secure good results. Unnecessary leniency, for instance, should be avoided. Barnes and Teeters observe that "there have been all too many cases in which there has been leniency in granting parole, but from a professional point of view sentiment should have no place in its dispensation."[34] Precautions are also necessary to ensure that parole is obtained not by money and political influence but by "good conduct, demonstration of ability to earn living honestly, and an attitude that promises success."[35] Else, the whole scheme would defeat its own purpose.

Both the parole officer and the parole board have significant role to play in the application of this correctional technique. It is the parole officer who is the "pivot" of the entire scheme. Supervision and guidance are his fundamental duties. He must understand the responsibility of supervision. "Supervision", as Barnes and Teeters correctly explain, "does not mean espionage ; the parole officer must not be a policeman. He should be a friend in need, an adviser who thoroughly understands the individual's peculiar problems arising from his term in prison. Many of these problems would not get a moment's though from the free citizen. The released prisoner must make hundreds of decisions each day that he did not make before release. Obtaining clothing, food, shelter, recreation, and catching up with the loose ends of the humdrum life of the average citizen are serious, complicated tasks".[36]

Parole being a form of conditional release the parolees are required to observe specified rules, such as abstaining from the use of narcotics and intoxicating liquors, keeping away from bad association, not carrying weapons, not visiting or corresponding with inmates of penal institutions, returning home by a stated hour in the evening (usually 10 p.m.), refraining from gambling, reporting promptly the loss of employment and so on. "It is no doubt possible", as Barnes and Teeters very aptly observe, "to justify these rules in many cases, but some of them make a day-by-day adjustment in a normal society extremely difficult... With adequately trained parole personnel reliance upon these rules will rarely be necessary. Scolding by the supervisor should be as infrequent as possible, and shadowing should never be necessary."[37] Needless to say, the appointment of the parole officer should be on "merit" and not 'political consideration" and that he should be well-paid and not overworked. "An untrained parole offlcer or an over-worked one", presumes Dr. B.K. Bhattacharya very aptly, "is likely to be slip-shod in his methods and is likely to bring into disrepute the whole system."[38]

An "intelligent", "public-spirited," and "progressive" parole board with "sufficient time at its disposal for dealing with individual cases" is of utmost importance. The majority of the members, if not all, should be full-time officials. The board should always give serious thought to the institutional record (to be furnished by the prison officials including welfare officer, psychologists and psychiatrists) of each and every prisoner who is to rejoin the mainstream of the community life. Like other parole personnel, the members of the parole board should also have adequate training.

Not only the parole officer or the parole board but the prison administrators as well have important role to play in the parole work. Even the most efficient parole board is bound to fail in discharging their duties effectively if they are not provided with necessary institutional records of the prisoners, carefully compiled by the prison personnel. For an efficient functioning of the parole system what is most necessary is alertness to the exact psychological moment when a man should be admitted to parole. For, as Barnes and Teeters observe, when the offender "exhibits those characteristics and behaviour patterns that indicate his sincere interest in going straight, and when his community assets are adequately mobilized for his reception, he should at once have parole privileges. To keep him longer breeds bitterness and may destroy all real desire to reform."[39]

Almost all prisoners including those with fixed, or with indeterminate sentences may be released through the parole procedure provided they are "adequately selected and efficiently supervised." Carefully selected recidivists even may have chance of success in parole.

These apart, the success of parole depends also on several other factors such as good neighbourhood, dependable home and associates, a job with good use of leisure time, etc.

As the prisons are even to-day the poorest place we could possibly provide for reformation or rehabilitation, the quicker we can get a man released from it, the better. A rational parole plan can help us to do this.[40] Unfortunately, in most of the states in India, the parole systems are very poorly organized despite several official committees having urged the governments to liberalize the procedures for premature release of prisoners on parole.

It should also be emphasized that the techniques of both probation and parole should be more liberally used in the case of juvenile delinquents. Unless unavoidable, they should not be awarded the sentence of imprisonment for their offence. Even when such sentences are inevitable, the delinquent juveniles under the age of sixteen must never be lodged in prisons, but diverted wholesale, as suggested by several prison reform committees including the West Bengal Jail Code Revision Committee of 1972-73, to confinement centres specially built for them such as Remand Homes, Certified Schools, Borstals, etc.

After-care of Released Prisoners

After-care of released prisoners as one of the most effective means to curb recidivism constitutes an integral part of correctional programmes. An offender, immediately after release from prison, has to confront with a lot of social and personal problems, such as loss of family contacts, lack of suitable employment opportunities, social stigma of prison sentence and so on. It is for a solution of these serious problems that a discharged offender needs community's solace, sympathy, help and care without which he will, in all probability, find no other alternative but to revert to crime. Absence of after-care, therefore, gives rise to recidivism.[41]

"After-care," to quote the Model Prison Manual, "is the released person's convalescence. It is the bridge which can carry him from the artificial and restricted environment of institutional custody, from doubts and difficulties, hesitations and handicaps to satisfactory citizenship, resettlement and to ultimate rehabilitation in the free community."[42]

The objects of after-care service, as stated in *Model Prison Manual*, are :

(a) to extend help, guidance, counselling, support and protection to all released prisoners whenever necessary,

(b) to help a released person to overcome his mental, social and economic difficulties,

(c) to help in the removal of any social stigma that may attach to the inmate or his family because of incarceration,

(d) to impress upon the individual the need to adjust his habits, attitudes, approaches and value schemes on a rational appreciation of social responsibilities and obligations and also of requirements of community living,

(e) to help the individual to make smooth physical, mental, social, and vocational adjustments with his post-release environment including his family, neighbourhood, work group and community,

(f) to assist the individual in functioning as a self-dependent and self-reliant socially useful citizen and in the process of his ultimate social rehabilitation.[43]

Despite the usefulness of after-care service, there has been very little progress in this major area of correctional activities in India. Some sporadic efforts to render a part of this service to the released offenders have, however, been made in some of the States. Yet, the actual aftercare work that has been done so far in this country "falls far too short of the requirements." Lack of funds, ignorance of the psychological and economic basis of crimes, and general apathy are the major factors standing in the way.

Needless to say, implementation of any useful programme depends very much on the availability of funds. It is, therefore, essential, at the outset, to remove financial obstacle if we really desire to bring about satisfactory improvement in after-care activities in our country. Otherwise, the enormous public money spent on the maintenance of prisoners tends to be a colossal waste. But, how to raise this money ?

The West Bengal Jail Code Revision Committee suggest that "public leaders and selfless social workers have to approach the affluent members of the community to contribute liberally to create something like a public charitable trust to finance the philanthropic activities of After-Care Associations in the State." The Committee further adds that "this is absolutely necessary in the interest of public security."[44]

It would be worthwhile in this connection to mention the Claude Martin Fund as a shining example of what the charity of a single noble soul can achieve by way of ameliorating the condition of many a hapless prisoner after release. This Fund which is administered by the Commissioner of Police, Calcutta has been in existence for over a hundred years, originating as it did form a deed of gift left by the estate of the late General Clude Martin with whose donations the La Martiniere School and College were founded at Calcutta and Lucknow. A lot of prisoners have since received financial assistance out of this fund to start a new life after release.

Creating public charitable trust, however, is not enough. The public should also be encouraged to render voluntary service in after-care activities either individually or under "the umbrella of an independent voluntary organization." The western experience of correctional work reveals that there is ample scope for work by voluntary agencies in the after-care of released prisoners. An ideal after-care scheme should begin at the commencement of sentence. Starting from interviews with offenders at the court immediately after sentence, the functions of voluntary agencies can be extended to a wide variety of programmes, such as group work with prisoners and their wives and families during sentence, looking after children during mother's v sit to prison, providing transport to prisons, support and advice to offenders and their families in their own homes after release, setting up of after-care hotels for accommodating homeless ex-prisoners, supportive work with homeless ex-prisoners living in lodgings or hostels, helping offenders to find employment and to take part in community life, etc.[45]

In the developed countries of the West, voluntary social and religious organizations have been doing a lot of extremely useful and humanitarian work pertaining to after-care of released prisoners. One such is the *New Bridge* in England which was set up more than two decades ago to help ex-prisoners find jobs. It has compiled for this purpose an index.

of prospective employers who are personally contacted for their cooperation. A body of volunteers has also been developed for establishing and maintaining contacts with employers and for interviewing candidates. Liaison with prisoners is maintained so that they may be interviewed prior to discharge.[46] In USA, the Friendly Visitors Incorporated, the Women Prison Association, the Issac T. Hopper Home and other institutions have been rendering valuable after-care services, such as counselling, guidance and advice, necessary for the self-development and social rehabilitation of released offenders.

In India, the Discharged Prisoners' Aid Society was established for the first time in Uttar Pradesh way back in 1894. Thereafter, such societies were set up in the then provinces of Madras, Central Provinces, Punjab, Bengal and Bombay between 1921 and 1933. Apart from helping the released prisoners in their social and economic rehabilitation, these societies also rendered invaluable service for reclamation of habitual offenders, prevention of casual and juvenile offenders from becoming habituals. But unfortunately, some of these societies have already been closed down for want of funds. adequate governmental support and recognition. Those which still exist are the U.P. Crime Prevention Society, All India Crime Prevention Society, Madras Discharged Prisoners' Aid Society and Maharashtra State Probation and After-care Association.[47] Emphasizing the need for revival of after-care programmes, the Mulla Committee suggested that efforts should be made to set up at least one voluntary organization in each district to which the work of extending help to released prisoners could be entrusted. "It should be the policy of the government," says the Committee, "to encourage formation of voluntary organisations for taking up programmes for the help of released prisoners. Such voluntary organizations should be given financial and other help to make it easier for them to carry on this work. Voluntary workers devoting considerable part of their leisure time to such work should be socially recognized,"[48]

Conclusion

We have discussed in this chapter two important subjects—capital punishment and social rehabilitation of prisoners—which are apparently diametrically opposed to each other, but are in reality swings of the same pendulum. Both of these are now matters of serious concern to the modern penologists and sensitive souls feel as if torn to two halves by their opposite pulls. Society has long been using capital punishment as a last resort to combat crime, but its efficacy as a deterrent has not yet been conclusively proved. Ironically, this inhuman, brutal and degrading type of punishment is still retained in the land of Buddha and Gandhi. Indian public sentiment has also not yet aroused against its retention despite a prolonged movement for its abolition by Jayaprakash Narayan, J.B. Kripalani and other distinguished Gandhians. However, it is heartening to note that the courts in India have been inflicting this extreme penalty with extreme infrequency so much so that the death penalty is not imposed now except in the rarest of rare cases. Yet, in view of the growing menace of organized violence and terrorist activities in this country it is too early to assume that the death penalty will be deleted from the statute book in near future. We have, therefore, considered the question whether our existing mode of execution by hanging need to be replaced by a more humane method. We suggest, after critical and comparative review of various methods of execution, that our existing laws should be amended to provide for three methods of execution—lethal injection, electrocution and hanging—so that the convict may decide for himself in which way he wants to die.

The problem of social rehabilitation of prisoners has been discussed in greater details and it is felt that in view of the failure of our existing prison system to reform criminals there is a need for increasing application of non-punitive and community-based treatment of offenders such as probation, parole and after-care. Various measures have been suggested to this direction.

NOTES AND REFERENCES

1. For further details see the *Report of the Royal Commission on Capital Punishment* (1949-53), H.M.S.O., London, Reprinted in 1973, Paragraph 50-68.
2. Harry Elmer Barnes and Negley K. Teeters, *New Horizons in Criminology*, Indian edn. 1966, p. 312.
3. 408 U.S. 238 (1972).
4. L.H. Hiranandani, "The Sentence of Death", *Illustrated Weekly*, August 29, 1976, p. 11.
5. Quoted by Hiranandani, *op. cit.*. pp. 8 and 15.
6. Jaytilak Guha Roy, "Humanizing the Mode of Execution', *The Statesman*, May 27, 1982.
7. Quoted by Hiranandani, *op. cit.*, pp. 14-15.
8. *Supra*, note 4, p. 12.
9. AIR 1973 SC 947 ; See also H.M. Seervai, *Constitutional Law of India*, 2nd edn., 1975, vol. I, p. 345.
10. e.g. Art. 72 (1)(c), Art. 134.
11. AIR 1980 SC 898.
12. *Supra*. note 4 at p. 15.
13. AIR 1951 SC 124.
14. *Supra*, note 6.
15. *Report of the Royal Commission on Capital Punishment*, *op. cit.*, Paragraph 709.
16. *Ibid.*, Paragraph 714.
17. Quoted by P.N. Bhagwati, J. in his minority decision in *Bachan Singh V. State of Punjab*, AIR, 1982 SC 1325 at p. 1347.
18. *Supra*, note 6.
19. *Report of the Royal Commission on Capital Punishment*, *op. cit.*,
20. *Ibid.*, Paragraph 738.
21. *Ibid.*, Paragraph 740.
22. *Supra*, note 6.

20. *Report of the Sixth United Nations Congress on the Prevention of Crime and Treatment of offenders*, p. 7.

24. Chamber of Commerce, U.S.A., *Marshalling Citizen Power to Modernize Corrections* (monograph), reprinted in 1972 by the American Correctional Association, p. 2.
25. *Supra*, note 23, pp. 12-13.
26. *Supra*, note 24, p. 6.
27. D.N. Ray, "The Probation Approach", *The Journal of Correctional Work*, No. XVII, 1971, p. 27.
28. M.A. Subramaniam. "How Probation can Reduce Recidivism, "*The Journal of Correctional Work*, No. XVII, 1971, p. 31.
29. Mahmood Bin Muhammad, while speaking on "Police and Probationers at a National Seminar on Probation ; see the Report of the

Seminar by J.J. Panakal, K.G. Dighe, Tata Institute of Social Science, Bombay, 1961, p. 18.

30. S.D. Singh, while speaking on "Law of Probation in India" at a National Seminar on Probation : see the Report of the Seminar, *Ibid.*, p. 22.
31. *Report*, p. 37.
32. Govt. of India : Ministry of Home Affairs, *Report of the All India Committee on Jail Reforms*, 1980-83 (Chairman : Justice A.N. Mulla), Vol. II, p. 261.
33. Edwin H. Sutherland, Donald R. Cressey, *Principles of Criminology*, 2nd Indian reprint, 1968, pp. 569-70.
34. Barnes and Teeters, *op. cit.*, pp. 567-68.
35. B K. Bhattacharya, *Prisons*, 1958, p. 111.
36. Barnes and Teeters, *op. cit.*, pp. 575-76.
37. *Ibid.*, p. 576.
38. B.K. Bhattacharya, *op. cit.*, p. 111.
39. Barnes and Teeteers, *op. cit.*, p. 382.
40. *Ibid.*
41. Jaytilak Guha Roy, "The Role of Public in the After-care of Discharged Offenders," *The Journal of Correctional Work*, No. XXIII, 1977, p. 73.
42. Govt. of India, *Model Prison Manual*, p. 264.
43. *Ibid.*, pp. 264-65.
44. Report of the Committee, p. 42.
45. *The Place of Voluntary Service in After-care* (Second Report of the Working Party, London), HMSO, 1967, p. 8.
46. Sudha Mazumdar, "Rehabilitattion of Female Offenders" (mimeographed).
47. S.P. Srivastava, *Public Participation in Social Defence*, 1981, pp. 73-74.
48. *Supra.*, note 32. p. 267.

9

RESTRUCTURING OF THE INDIAN PRISON ADMINISTRATION

In the preceding chapters the principles, purposes and the methods of modern correctional treatment and the actual operation of prisons in India have been discussed. The concluding chapter is a modest endeavour to shed light on various aspects of administrative reorganization of the Indian jail system with a view to materializing these principles and purposes.

There are three principal perspectives for determining the reorganization scheme for any prison system. These are : (i) humanitarianism, (ii) social rehabilitation, and (iii) the actual financial capacity of the government which limits feasibility of the scheme. The principles of humanitarianism and social rahabilitation are now being applied in many countries as far as possible. But, the feasibility of the scheme, that is, how much of humanitarianism land how much social rehabilitation can be accepted as governing principles of jail administration, depends much on the financial capacity of the government, which is the most practical consideration. Financial perspective is a restraining element, whereas the other two are idealistic, though progressive forces. Thus, while formulating the policy for jail admistration, the policy-maker, whether as a person or as a body, must have a balanced as well as an integrated view of which the importance of each of the above three perspectives are given due weightage. This essentially calls for involvement of allied agencies and departments in the decision-making process of the prison department.

After having formed a clear idea of the relative importance of the three principal perspectives that should govern any scheme of prison reorganization, we may now proceed to our analysis and assessment of the elements that constitute the structural core of jail administration in India.

Organization

The success and purposiveness of any enterprise rests upon its organization. As has been well said that "while organization is the structuring of individuals and functions into productive relationship, administration is concerned with decision making and the direction of individuals to achieve ends that have been determined by political leaders." Organization, therefore, seeks a pattern of skills and responsibilities that ensure coordination and unity of purpose through supervision. But the object of both, organization and administration, is to control human and material resources, so that the end may be realized with minimum cost of time, energy and money.[1]

Organizational efficiency depends largely on planning. Planning involves systematic thinking about ends and means together. Thinking of the ends ought to be rational. Choice of means is difficult since there are various means for a single end. L. Urwick observes that every organization is concerned with "determining what activities are necessary to any purpose (or plan) and arranging them in groups which may be assigned to individuals." This is the 'structural' approach which has been criticized by modern behaviourists and socio-psychologists on the ground that it does not take into account the role of the individual in the organization but rather emphasizes the tasks to be performed by the individuals attached to it.

Herbert A. Simon, the most eminent exponent of the 'contemporary' approach, holds that as the individual is the centre of activities of an organization, he has to play a significant role in its functioning. Consequently, the organization takes the form of not merely a structure of charts, diagrams or instructions, but also of a cooperative human activity. Human resources, cooperative efforts, and a common purpose are thus the three principal elements of an organization.[2]

Prison reforms in India during the post-Independence period were primarily confined to improving the living conditions of prisoners with little or no regard either for their reformative and rehabilitative needs or for rationalization of organizational structure. The existing organizational set up of jail administration in this country which is by and large the creation of the alien rulers is comprised of two divisions : (i) Headquarters Organization, and (ii) Institutional Organization.

Headquarters Organization

The Prison Department in all the States functions under the Home Department which, as is well-known, deals with law and order. In some States such as West Bengal there is a separate division of the Home Department for dealing with jail administration. The jurisdiction as well as the organizational pattern of the Prison Departments vary from State to State. As the Government of India's Working Group of 1972-73 have observed, "This is due mainly to the fact that the prisons being exclusively under the State jurisdiction, the State Governments have developed and expanded their Prison Departments according to their local conditions and available resources" [3]

In the present organizational structure there is lack of coordination between the activities of prison services and allied correctional services such as services under the Probation Act and the Juvenile Justice Act. With the creation of Social Welfare Departments the probation and women and juvenile corrections have been transferred to separate departments in some States. In Gujarat and Karnataka, for instance, these services are now dealt with by the Department of Social Defence and the Director of Women and Child Welfare respectively. Likewise, in Tamil Nadu the juvenile correctional institutions are administered by the Home Department. On the contrary, in a number of States, Viz.. Andhra Pradesh,

Bihar, Haryana, Himachal Pradesh, Maharashtra, Punjab, Tamil Nadu and West Bengal, the work of probation which is a non-institutional technique for treatment of offenders continues to have been handled by the prison departments which are primarily concerned with institutional treatment of offenders. Consequently, barring the transfer of case-loads from one department to the other, there has been, in fact, no coordination between prison and probation services. The development of the probation system is also retarded under this organizational structure since for almost every matter concerning probation, the profation authority is to take instructions from the prison department which is already overburdened with its heavy load of work pertaining to prison services and has practically little or no time to deal with other correctional services such as probation. It is, therefore, necessary to recognize the existing structure of the headquarters organization in such a manner that different branches of correctional services, viz., prisons, probation, women and juvenile corrections, may function as separate Directorate independently of each other but are at the same time, integrated and brought under "one umbrella". Keeping in view that the principal job of the correctional personnel will be the social re-education of the offender, the West Bengal Jail Code Revision Committee (1972-73) has proposed a completely new set-up (as shown under Chart 1) for the Headquarters organization which, it hopes, 'would be able to awaken in the minds of the personnel the conviction that correctional work is a social service of great importance."[4]

Under the proposed set-up for the Headquarters organization, social welfare (i.e. women and juvenile corrections, etc.) and probation have been sought to be integrated with prison administration. To quote the report of this Committee,[5] "All these (services) apparently appear to be different, but they really aim at the same objective, namely, dealing with social hazards created mainly by the socio-economic condition in the country . . . To reap the maximum benefits through one integrated plan, the Committee has decided to recommend the appointment of one Senior Officer at the top of the administration of these three Directorates. It has suggested to give him

CHART 1

Structure of Headquarters Organization for Correctional Services as proposed by the West Bengal Jail Code Revision Committee of 1972-73

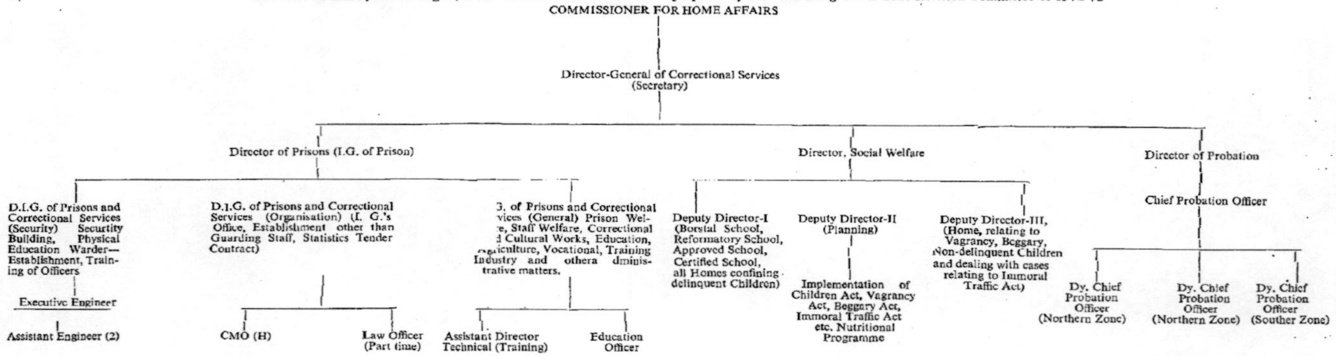

the rank of a Secretary under the Commissioner for Home Affairs. The Committee is of the view that this officer will not only be able to relieve the Home Commissioner of his heavy load of work but will also be able to do justice to the huge responsibility of reeducating the socially handicapped persons to fit them properly in civil society."

There is hardly any doubt that prison and allied correctional services, if restructured in line with the proposed scheme and properly manned, will facilitate "an integrated approach to the treatment of offenders". It is, however, difficult to give the Director General (D.G.) of Correctional Services the rank of a Secretary as suggested by this Committee since this cannot be done without restructuring the entire state administrative system. What seems to be more practical and desirable is that like the D.G., Police, the D.G., Correctional Services should also be appointed from senior and experienced officers of the prison department and not from the IAS, IPS or Medical Services as has now been the practice for the appointment of the Inspector General of Prisons in some States. In large States there is also need for delegation of authority to officers at regional level, as suggested by Justice Mulla Committee,[6] not only to relieve the officers of the Headquarters organization of their heavy load of day-to-day work but also to enable them to provide effective supervision, control and direction.

Institutional Organization

The institutional set-up of prisons consists of various types of institutions ranging from central prisons to district/sub-jails. The district jails are further divided into various classes on the basis of the size of the district and the strength of inmate population. Each of these different types of prisons is headed by a superintendent. There are ordinarily three grades of superintendents : superintendents of central prisons, whole-time superintendents of bigger districts jails, part-time superintendents of smaller district jails and/or sub-jails in the tehsils/taluks/sub-divisions of districts. Several official committees including the Indian Jails Committee of 1919-20 time and again objected to the appointment of medical officers as part-time superintendents. Yet, in smaller districts in many States, Civil Surgeons still continue to be employed as part-time superintendents. This system suffers from several handicaps since the superintendent holds a key position in the internal administration of jails and thereby assumes onerous administrative responsibilities which the Civil Surgeons are unable to accomplish in addition to their medical duties. As the Working Group of 1972-73 pertinently observed : "They can, as best, pay hasty visits, leaving the administration entirely in the hands of the jailors. They find it physically impossible to exercise regular supervision and control over the various prison operations, nor they adequately equipped to deal with the intricate problems of the prison administration". The Group have, therefore, recommended that all district jails with an average population of 300 prisoners or more should be headed by whole-time superintendents specially trained and equipped to perform their duties and that deputy superintendents may be appointed in central prisons and in district jails which have an inmate strength of the level of central prisons.[7]

The sub-jails are, at present, placed in several states, under the control of part-time superintendents from the Medical, Revenue or Judicial Departments and are guarded by policemen. If the general conditions in central or district jails are bad, those of the sub-jails are even worse. Apart from the inability of part-time superintendents to devote adequate time and attention to the supervision of sub-jails, the present state of affairs is also due to lack of provision for higher level inspection and control by officers of the Prison Department. As the Working Group of 1972-73 observed : "An offender, whether guilty of a criminal offence or involved in a political or other agitation, is first lodged in a sub-jail in all places (tehsils/taluks/sub-divisions of district) other than the district headquarters. It is desirable, therefore, that his first experience of jails custody should not be such as to bring discredit to the entire penal system of the country. It follows that a planned and systematic improvement of the sub-jails all over the country should be an item of high priority in jail reforms. . . We consider it necessary, therefore, that all sub-jails suould be provided with a full-time superintendent of the jail cadre of appropriate rank and an adequate number of warder staff for custodial duty. Such an arrangement will bring the sub jails under the inspection and control of the district and regional officers of the Prison Departments."[8]

The medical administration of the jails also needs to be reorganized. In a number of States such as West Bengal the medical officers are drawn in on loan or deputation from the Health Departments and consequently, the Prison Departments often do not get the quality of service they deserve from these officers. It is, therefore, necessary to create completely separate and independent cadre of Medical Services under the Prison Departments instead of manning the services by officers from the Health Departments.[9]

Under the present set-up of institutional organisation, the welfare activities in jails are ordinarily not separated from the general administration for which the Welfare Officers do not hold adequate powers to discharge their duties and responsibilities independently. It is, therefore, essential in order to enable these officers to perform their duties properly that welfare services in jails are separated from the general administration and that the detailed nature and scope of their duties, responsibilities and powers are codified. These officers should also be provided with adequate promotional opportunities, and this can be done if the posts of Director and Deputy Director, Social Welfare are created and filled in from amongst them on the basis of seniority and professional ability.

It must, however, be borne in mind that no real improvement in the present set-up of prison organization in India is possible without reorganizing the jail department for a career service. Way back in 1951-52, the U.N. expert, Dr. Walter C. Reckless, observed in his report on *Jail Administration in India* that if jails were going to be rehabilitation centres, we had to have men at the top who had the experience, the knowledge and the skill. He, therefore, recommended that the jail service should be a career service and that officers of this service should man all posts including the top posts in the prison department.[10] Subsequently, several official committees including the latest Justice Mulla Committee poignantly observes : "The very fact that out of 22 States and 9 Union Territories only 3 States have departmentally promoted Inspectors General of Prisons while the rest have Inspectors General appointed from other services, points to the poor attention paid to the development of prison service as a career service in the country. Senior posts of Additional Inspector General, Deputy Inspector General and even Superintendents of central prisons in several states are reported to have been lying vacant as departmental candidates eligible or fit for promotion to these posts are either not available or, if available, are not being promoted for one reason or the other."[11] It is now high time that jail service becomes a career service and a "specialized profession" having adequate promotional avenues.

Staff

The successful implementation of correctional programmes for the prisoners mainly depends on the quality of the prison staff at various levels. Staff matters, in general, include three important elements : recruitment, salary and promot ion.

"Recruitment", to quote Professor Bhambri, "means the efforts to find out and induce suitable candidates to compete for appointment to the public service . . . A bad policy of recruitment can wreck the entire personnel programme. Any country which wants to have efficient personnel for public services must have a sound and scientific policy of recruitment."[12]

Proper man-power planning is *sine qua non* for a sound and scientific policy of recruitment. While the work-load and the strength of various cardes in the prison service may differ from State to State according to their size and crime situation, man-power planning for the future organization of prison department in each State/Union Territory has to be done keeping in view the multi-dimensional role of this department in respect of institutional treatment, probation and after-care of adult and young offenders.[13] There should also be properly constituted Recruitment and Selection Boards in State/Union Territory Public Service Commissions for selection and recruitment of efficient and suitable personnel for these services. The Boards should consist of experienced prison administrators, social workers, criminologists and psychologists. To quote the report of the Working Group of 1972-73. "The selectors of personnel in this area of public administration, as in the other uniformed sevices, have to look for physical fitness and courage, leadership and non-management qualities as well as the dependability which is guaranteed by a balanced personality. In addition they will have to look for endurance qualities, a broad interest in social welfare and a flair for human relationship."[14]

The availability of efficient and suitably qualified personnel depends much on salaries and other employment benefits. "Salaries and other employment benefits", as suggested by the *Model Prison Manual* (1960) "should not be arbitrarily fixed but should be related to the work to be performed in a modern correctional system, which is complex and arduous and is in the nature of an important social service. The correctional staff should be paid salary sufficient to secure and retain faithful service. Conditions of service should afford necessary safe-guards against risks and handicaps involved in the service."[15]

Unfortunately till now the prison and correctional personnel in most of the States and Union Territories are not paid adequate salary commensurate with the responsibilities attached to their work. They are even deprived of certain necessary employment benefits such as subsidised rationing and accommodation facilities, extended to the personnel of their complenentary service, namely, the police service, with the result that "prison service holds very little prospect to ambitious young men of good education and dependable integrity."[16] These deficiencies of prison service have been clearly brought out by Dr. Reckless in his following observation contained in his report to the Government of India :

"The expert has the distinct feeling that the jail department of India, as is true elsewhere, is a disadvantaged department. No Secretary is really interested in jails. The police get the lion's share of Government consideration, because of Internal security. Government and public many times look upon jail administration as corrupt and brutal. The department is likely to get bottom consideration in the priority list. The jail officials feel that they are definitely disadvantaged in conditions of service as against the police, especially in pay scale. The Conference of Inspectors-General of Prisons asked for equalisation of related pay scale and cadres of service. Even though the expert is naturally biased toward to development of a fine jail department there is much truth in the assertion that jail department should have higher status in Government than police department, because jails can do, if given the opportunity, a constructive job of rehabilitation."

Thus, in order to "facilitate recruitment of really dependable men to administer the prisons along right lines," equailisation of related pay scales and cadres of both the police and the prison services is of utmost importance. Necessary employment benefits given to the police presonnel in some States should also be extended to the personnel of prison and correctional services. "Expenditure on staff welfare and amenities," as the Report of the West Bengal Jail Code Revision of 1972-73 has very pertinently observed, "should be considered as well spent. The conventional idea of running the prisons in as cheap a manner as possible should be dismissed though economy in expenditure in all possible ways should be enforced without affecting the efficiency of administration in any way."[17]

Finally, the existing condition of prison service in respect of work-load and duty hours of the personel should necessarily be improved. The prison executives and their assistants and other guarding staff are now to spend the better part of their duty hours not in "intensive personal work with the prisoner" for whose welfare they are recruited and paid from the public exchequer, but in "just administrative and clerical work on the one hand and policing work in the yards of the prison on the other." To quote Dr. Reckless. "It would be just as if the sisters or nurses of a hospital and the doctors had no time for patients but merely kept books and saw to it that they stayed in bed."[18]

Another important element of staff matters is promotion. Promotion actually means "rise to a higher grade, a new salary-scale, with change in responsibilities and duties." It is a continuous incentive to efficient working on the part of the employee, provided it is based on a "well-developed" policy. The advantages of a well-developed promotion policy are :

(i) It keeps the personnel efficient.
(ii) It ensures rewards for efficient service.
(iii) It helps to attract qualified people towards the service as they know that opportunities exist for progress.
(iv) It enables the employer to fill the higher and responsible posts from the experienced and capable persons who are already in the service.[19]

The Working Group of 1972-73 observed that there was considerable diversity in the admission of direct recruits and the level and percentages of their entry, vis-a-vis promotees and transferees from State to State. Unfortunately, due to political and bureaucratic apathy to prison administration, such diversity still persists and there is a need for rationalizing the system of recruitment and promotion on an acceptable and reasonably uniform basis throughout India. Direct entry into the prison service, as recommended by this Group, should be restricted to only three levels viz., Warder Grade II, Assistant Jailor and the lowest level of the Superintendent's Cadre by whatever name it is called. The direct recruitment quota in the last two categories should be fixed at 50% while the other 50% should be filled mainly through departmental promotion. The Group also suggested that all direct recruitment to the posts of Deputy Jailor, Jailor and the Superintendent of Higher rank should be reserved exclusively for promotion.[20] There is also the need for developing an ideal system of promotion for prison personnel. Promotion to higher cadres should be based on seniority as well as the systematic and objective evaluation of the incumbent's merit, professional aptitude, integrity, devotion to the job and trustworthiness rather than on seniority alone.

Training of Personnel

The training of personnel is of paramount importance in a system of scientific prison administration of modern times. As the report of the West Bengal Jail Code Revision Committee (1972-73) has aptly observed, "Modern prison administration is a highly specialized professional job just as looking after a modern hospital is a highly specialized professional job. The most important job in a correctional institution is to re-educate, retrain and rebuild the personality of the prisoner. Only a prison personnel, especially trained for the job and genuinely devoted to the cause of reclamation and rehabilitation of prisoners, can lead them to the cherished goal."[21]

A properly trained staff will always be an asset in the effective implementation of correctional policies and programmes. "With impacts of training, the attitudes and abilities of the personnel will improve. The expenditure incurred for staff training will ultimately result not only in departmental gains but also in social gains in terms of better institutional impacts and ultimate rehabilitation of the offenders."[22]

The ultimate object of staff training programmes should be to reflect the social realities surrounding the administration. According to *Model Prison Manual*, training programmes for correctional personnel should aim at :

(i) acquainting correctional personnel with scientific and progressive methods of correctional Administration ;

(ii) making them conscious of their responsibilities and also of the role they have to play in a welfare state ;

(iii) broadening of their cultural and professional interests ; experience ; refining their abilities and skills ; improving their performance of administrative duties ; providing them with experience to meet future needs of the department in positions of higher responsibilities and

(iv) inculcating an *esprit-de-corps* amongst the correctional personnel.[23]

Training programmes for personnel in most of the States in India have not yet developed in accordance with the objectives of modern correctional administration. It is disheartening to note that much emphasis is still now being given on the security-based training of the prison personnel rather than on training in correctional work. In view of continuous failure of our prison system in reformation of offenders, there is a growing need for redesigning the training programmes for prison personnel with the objects of preparing them for their specialized job which is not merely custodial but also correctional in nature.

Training programmes, however, cannot be organized effectively without a compact Training School. The functions of compact training Institute, according to *Model Prison Manual*, should be : (i) training, (ii) research, (iii) methods and organization work, and (iv) publication of pamphlets, papers, handbooks, correctional journal, etc.[24] Surprisingly, in India there are now only 3 training institutions (at Lucknow, Pune and Vellore) for the training of officers of the prison department and only 11 for the training of lower staff, when the number of prisons in the country is 1220 and that of prison personnel 27,646. Even these few institutions are not properly equipped to cater to the training needs to prison personnel. Justice Mulla Committee has, therefore, emphasized the need for setting up proper training institutions at state, regional and the national level. While training to the security staff should be imparted at State level, training institutes for officers at the executive level should be established at the regional level catering to the needs of a group of States and Union Territories. The Committee have also suggested that the Central Government should establish a training institute at the national level to meet the training needs of senior officers. Apart from imparting training in policy formulation, planning and various aspects of management, this institute is also expected to play a useful role in imparting an all India perspective of the development of prisons and other correctional services to these officers.[25] Curriculum for these training programmes should be carefully drawn up keeping in view the broad objectives of modern correctional administration and the training needs of each particular group of participants.

Finally, since training is a continuous process, the pre-service training imparted at the Correetional Training School needs to be continued at the institutional level. It has, therefore, been rightly suggested by the *Model Prison Manual* that suitable training programmes should be or ganized at the institution so that the institutional personnel may constantly remain acquainted with current developments in the field of corrections. According to the *Manual* the following training facilities should be provided at the institutions ;

(i) interpretation of policy by senior officers from Head-Quarters during visits ;
(ii) library and reading room facilities for staff members :
(iii) lectures by Professors from the Universities or Schools or Social Work on subjects related with correctional work ;
(iv) fortnightly talk on correctional methods by the superintendent or any other senior officer ;
(v) reading of papers, case histories, etc. by institutional personnel ;
(iv) monthly discussions on improvement in administrative procedures, methods and organization. etc.[26]

Coordination

The successful implementation of any administrative programme depends very much on the co-ordination of the activities of various parts of the organisation. To quote J.C. Charlesworth, "Coordination is the integration of the several parts into an orderly whole to achieve the purpose of the undertaking."[27]

Coordination, however, involves difficult and delicate exercise of administrative skills and techniques. In India, "the greatest hindrance in the way of co-ordination," as Prof. Bhambri has aptly pointed out, "is lack of a sense of common purpose among the members of the organization. The head of the organization has to see to it that this positive spirit is created among the members. Many times emotional appeals are necessary to evoke individual loyalty." "Further," as he says, "specialists in an organization overemphasize their role and breed fragmentation in an organization. This splintering tendency of the specialists has to be checked by effective machinery of coordination."[28] In the same strain says Pfiffner-Presthus : "Coordination, then, is a technique for drawing together a number of conflicting skills and interests and leading them towards a common end. It is the centripetal force in administration."[29]

For jail administration, three types of coordination are required : (i) Intra-departmental, (ii) Interdepartmental, and (iii) Inter-State. Intra-departmental coordination can be achieved through formal methods, i.e., through "the commands, orders, instructions and directions" of the formal higher authority of the department. There is also the need for periodical meetings of the concerned officials of the department at various levels to discuss problems of common interest. Inter-departmental coordination, on the other hand, is sought to be achieved through other devices, viz., work-shops, conferences, inter-departmental-committees, periodical meetings of the higher authorities of related departments, etc. Since prison and correctional services are an integral part of the entire criminal justice system the development of these services can hardly be achieved without inter-departmental coordination of the activities of related departments such as police and judiciary. The problem of overcrowding in prisons for instance, cannot be solved even with the best efforts of the prison department unless the police and the judiciary extend full cooperation in disposing off pending cases.

Finally, since prison administration is a state subject under the Constitution of India, there is a need for Inter-state coordination too in order to ensure a unified and integrated development of prison services in this country. Periodical meetings or conferences of Chief Secretaries, Home Ministers and Secretaries, the Inspectors-General of Prisons of the different States and specialized coordinating agencies of the Central Government are some of the devices for achieving inter-state coordination. Central agencies like the National Institute of Social Defence will also be "useful avenue for exchange of information in regard to correctional matters" at the inter-state as well as the international levels provided necessary cooperation is extended to them by the Central and State Governments. Such agencies may also help "to coordinate the work and develop a uniform policy as far as possible in the different states with regard to prevention of crime and treatment of offenders."[30]

Budgeting

The supreme importance of budgeting is that it helps us to understand the ways in which an organization or a department functions, whether the funds available are sufficient for the work, whether they are being wasted or properly spent, whether there is any impending financial shortage or not.

According to one authority, "budgeting generally denotes the process by which the financial policy of a public agency is formulated, enacted and carried out".[31] Budget is a "plan of action," an aid to management. More elaborately, it is "a systematic method of gathering information from the past and present, of formulating plans for the future on the basis of this, and of reporting subsequently how these plans have been carried out."[32]

Budgeting for jail administration cannot be compared with industrial budget but rather with educational budget, for in jail budgeting the outputs i.e., character, behaviour etc., donot have any material value.

Estimates of expenditure constitute the most important part of budgeting. Jail expenditures can be divided into two parts : (i) expenditures that are absolutely necessary for social security, and (ii) expenditures which are meant to preserve culture and to promote humanitarianism among the prison population and the general public. Increasing the height of the prison wall, for instance, is an item of expenditure which is related to social security measures, while the expenditure for making gardens for prisoner's entertainment falls under the second category. Since the basic duties of a government are to ensure peace and security for its citizens the first category of expenditure should always be given priority. This does not, however, mean that the expenditure towards the improvement of prison conditions are to be considered as wasteful or unnecessary expenditure.

Expenditure on prisoners' diet needs also to be determined on the basis of specified standards and norms since a substantial part of the jail budget is spent for this purpose. The existing Jail Codes of a number of States and Union Territories provide for classified diets for different categories of prisoners. Determining the criteria for classified diets, however, involves a lot of problems. In earlier times two bases were adopted for such classification : (i) enormity of the crime committed, and (ii) the social class that the criminal comes from. It is very difficult to determine the enormity of the crime with any scientific precision. Take for instance the murder for robing five rupees from a person or murder for changing a government. Although the motive for the crime is different in these two cases, the enormity of the crime does not really vary for such differences, for every murder is a murder and an offence against society, no matter what is the motive for it. It would, therefore, be utterly unjustified to adopt enormity of the crime as the basis of any classification of prisoners' diet.

Moreover, classification of diets, either on the basis of enormity of the crime or of social status, is quite arbitrary, as it is not supported by any rational consideration. On the other hand, it is obvious that princely diets cannot be given to any prisoner under any consideration. The part of the budget that meets the costs of diet has, therefore, to be based upon strong common sense.

Preparation of budget estimates for the jail administration is not at all an easy task for the reasons that there are abrupt and frequent variations in prison population and also the contract-rates for supply of prisoners' food and other essential commodities. The problem will be even more acute where there is no provision for a reserve fund from which unexpected but necessary expenditures can be met the tide over temporary difficulties.

A cursory glance at the budget estimates of the past few years for jail administration in West Bengal and the all-India price index figures for working class during the corresponding periods (Tables . . . 11 and. . . 12) will enable us to understand the practical difficulties with which the planners and the policy makers of jail administration are often to confront with.

TABLE 11

All-India Consumer Price Index Numbers for Working Class*

	Food Index 1949=100	General Index 1949=100
Financial year		
1955-56	94	96
1960-61	125	124
1965-66	174	169
1966-67	198	191
1967-68	228	213
1968-69	223**	212**
1969-70	223	215
1970-71	233	216
1971-72	237	233
1972-73	258	251
1973-74	323	304

* Source : *Economic Survey*, 1974-75, Govt. of India p. 93.

** Based on four months' figures in the interim series (1949=100) and eight months' figures as estimated from the new series of Index on base 1960=100.

Assuming 100 to be the base of food index and general index in 1949, the food and general index figures rose from 94 and 96 in 1955-56 to 323 and 304 respectively in 1973-74 (see Table 11), while the jail expenditure (Table 12), rose from Rs, 84.94 lakhs in 1955-56 to 4.43 crores in 1975-76 and Rs. 5.76 crores in 1979-80. This reveals that although the jail expenditure in terms of money increased more than five time during the period of two decades (1956-76), the increase in real terms was negligible taking into account the rise in all-India consumer price index figures for the same period. As regards the standard of living of the unfortunate prisoners the statistics disclose even more miserable state of affairs. For, the daily average prison population itself went up from 11,953.32 in 1957 to 22,962 1976-77[33]. In terms of money too, the per capita expenditure on prison population increased

TABLE 12

Expenditure on Jail as per Budget Estimates of the Government of West Bengal

Head of Accounts	FINANCIAL YEARS				Head of Accounts	Financial year	
	1955-56	1960-61	1965-66	1971-72		1975-76	1979-80
	Rs. in Lakh	Rs. in Lakh	Rs. in Lakh	Rs. in Lakh		Rs. in Lakh	Rs. in Lakh
I. JAILS Pay of officers, establishments, contingencies, establishment to other Govt. deptts., etc.	86.29	99.00	120.81	228.845	I. Direction and Administration. (i.e. Salaries, pay, D.A., payment of professional & social services etc.)	4.25	7.00
II. JAIL MANUFACTURES Pay of officers, establishment, contingencies etc.	11.95	14.09	19.10	28.665	II. JAILS i.e. Salaries, pay, allowance directory changes, rent, taxes Grants in aid/ Contributions etc.	396.65	502.53
III. WORKS	—	—	0.14	—	III. Jail Manufactures (i.e. Pay, D.A., Materials and supplies, tools and plants, etc.)	34.794	41.38

IV. Lump provision for medical benefit	—	—	.2.40	—	IV. Other Expenditure (Salaries etc. of the establishment of jail schools, changes for moving prisoners, for police custody etc.)	23.586	42.30
V. Lump provision for Addl. D.A.	—	—	2.50	—			
VI. Lump Provision for Revision of pay scale	—	—	—	5.880			
GRAND TOTAL (Gross)	98.24	113.09	144.95	263.39		459.28	593.21
Deduct-Recoveries	13.30	9.01	14.10	15.10		16.00	17.00
GRAND TOTAL (Net)	84.94	104.08	130.85	248.29		443.28	576.21

from Rs. 2 per day in 1957 to Rs. 3.20 in 1971 and Rs. 6.03 in 1976-77,[34] while the all-India consumer price index figures for working class during this period rose from 96 in 1955-56 to 226 in 1970-71 and 304 in 1973-74 and further in later years. In plain language the prisoner is now getting poorer quality of diet, clothing and bedding than he used to in 1957.

Conclusion

We have discussed in this chapter various important measures for restructuring of the antediluvian Indian jail system. It is felt that if the prison or correctional service which has now become a highly specialized profession is to be organized as a career service, plan funds should be available for training and development of prison personnel. Other necessary programmes for prison reforms such as programmes for reformation and rehabilitation of offenders, functional renovation of old prison buildings, construction of new prison buildings and staff quarters, modernization/mechanization of prison industry and agriculture should also find place under the plan sector.[35] It should, however, be pointed out that prison and correctional administration is only one of the major components of the entire criminal justice system and hence, in the ultimate analysis, the enduring solution to the growing problems of jail administration would hinge on the political will and the administrative wisdom to bring about many-pronged reforms in all the sectors of criminal justice system—police, judiciary and correctional services.

NOTES AND REFERENCES

1. Pfiffner—Presthus, *Public Administration*, 4th edn., 1960, p. 5.
2. For further details on the traditional and contemporary approach to organization, see Herbert A. Simon, *Administrative Behaviour*, pp. 79-109.
3. Govt. of India : Ministry of Home Affairs, *Report of the Working Group on Prisons in the Country*, 1972-73 (mimeographed), p. 42.
4. Govt. of West Bengal : Home (Jails) Deptt., *Report of the Jail Code Revision Committee*, 1972-73, p. 15.
5. *Ibid.*, pp. 15-16.

6. Govt. of India : Ministry of Home Affairs, *Report of the All India Committee on Jail Reforms*, 1980-83, Vol. II. p. 271.
7. *Supra*. note 3, pp. 48-49.
8. *Supra*. note 3, pp. 49-50.
9. *Supra*. note 4, p. 61.
10. Walter C. Reckless, *Jail Administration in India* (mimeographed).
11. *Supra*. note 6, p. 278.
12. C.P. Bhambri, *Public Administration : Theory and Practice*, Third rev. edn., 1967, part III, p. 42.
13. *Supra*. note 6, p. 279.
14. *Supra*. note 3, p. 77.
15. Govt. of India, *Model Prison Manual*, p. 67.
16. *Supra*. note 4, p. 22.
17. *Supra*. note 4, p. 21.
18. *Supra*. note 10.
19. C.P. Bhambri, *op. cit.*, Part II, p. 88 ; M.P. Sharma, *Public Administration in Theory and Practice* pp. 360-375.
20. *Supra*. note 3, pp. 77-79.
21. *Supra*. note 4, p. 48.
22. Govt. of India, *Model Prison Manual*, 1960, p. 58.
23. *Ibid.*, p. 57.
24. *Ibid.*, p. 58.
25. *Supra*. note 6, pp. 285-86.
26. Govt. of India, *Model Prison Manual*, pp. 58, 64-65.
27. J.C. Charlesworth, *Governmental Administration*, New York, 1951.
28. C.P. Bhambri, *op. cit.*, Part I, p. 58.
29. Pfiffner—Presthus, *Public Administration*, 4th edn., 1960, p. 5.
30. Govt. of India, *Model Prison Manual*, Chap. V. Rule 7.
31. Joseph Pois, *Report of Financial Administration in the Michigan State Government*, Public Administration Service, Chicago, 1938, p. 67.
32. New York Policy holders Service Bureau : Metropolitan life Insurance Co., *The Budget as an Aid to Management*, 1940, p. 1.
33. Govt. of West Bengal, *Report on the Administration of Jails and Borstal School*, 1958 p. 2 ; Govt. of India, *Report of the Seventh Finance Commission*, 1977-78, Appendix V. 11 (ii).
34. Figures collected from the Prisons Directorate, Govt. of West Bengal and the Report of the Seventh Finance Commission.
35. For details see the Report of the All India Committee on Jail Reforms, 1980-83. Vol. II, Ch. XXV.

APPENDIX

DRAFT OF A NATIONAL POLICY ON PRISONS FORMULATED BY THE ALL INDIA COMMITTEE ON JAIL REFORMS OF 1980-83

Goals and Objectives

1. Prisons in the country shall protect society and shall endeavour to reform and reassimilate offenders in the social milieu by giving them appropriate correctional treatment.

Modalities

2. The State shall endeavour to bring about basic uniformity in the minimum standards of management of prisons and the treatment of offenders in the country through :

(i) incorporation of the principles of management of prisons and treatment of offenders in the Directive Principles of the State Policy embodied in Part IV of the Constitution of India :

(ii) inclusion of the subject of prisons and allied institutions in the Concurrent List of the Seventh Schedule to the Constitution of India ; and

(iii) enactment of uniform and comprehensive legislation embodying modern principles and procedures regarding reformation and rehabilitation of offenders.

3. There shall be in each State and Union Territory, a Department of Prisons and Correctional Services dealing with adult and young offenders—their institutional care, treatment, aftercare, probation and other non-institutional services.

4. The State shall endeavour to evolve proper mechanism to ensure that no undertrial prisoner is unnecessarily detained This shall be achieved by speeding up trials, simplification of bail procedures and periodic review of cases of undertrial prisoners. Undertrial prisoners shall, as far as possible, be confined in separate institutions.

5. Since it is recognised that imprisonment is not always the best way to meet the objectives of punishment the government shall endeavour to provide in law new alternatives to imprisonment such community service, forfeiture of property, payment of compensation to victims, public censure, etc., in addition to the ones already existing, and shall specially ensure that the Probation of Offenders Act, 1958 is effectively implemented throughout the country.

6. Living conditions in every prison and allied institution meant for the custody, care, treatment and rehabilitation of offenders shall be compatible with human dignity in all aspects such as accommodation, hygiene, sanitation, food, clothing, medical facilities, etc. All factors responsible for vitiating the atmosphere of these institutions shall be identified and dealt with effectively.

7. In consonance with goals and objectives of prisons, the State shall provide appropriate facilities and professional personnel for the classification of prisoners on a scientific basis. Diversified institutions shall be provided for the segregation of different categories of inmates for proper treatment.

8. The State shall endeavour to develop the fields of criminology and penology and promote research on the typology of crime in the context of emerging patterns of crime in the country. This will help in proper classification of offenders and in devising appropriate treatment for them.

9. A system of graded custody ranging from special security institutions to open institutions shall be provided to offer proper opportunities for the reformation of offenders according to the progress made by them.

10. Programmes for the treatment of offenders shall be individualised and shall aim at providing them with opportunities for diversified education, development of work habits and skills, change in attitude, modification of behaviour and implantation of social and moral values.

11. The State shall endeavour to develop vocational training and work programmes in prisons for all inmates eligible to work. The aim of such training and work programmes shall be to equip inmates with better skills and work habits for their rehabilitation.

12. Payment of fair wages and other incentives shall be associated with work programmes to encourage inmates participation in such programmes. The incentives of leave, remission and premature release to convicts shall also be utilised for improvement of their behaviour, strengthening, of family ties and their early return to society.

13. Custody being the basic function of prisons, appropriate security arrangements shall be made in accordance with the need for graded custody in different types of institutions. The management of prisons shall be characterised by firm and positive discipline, with due regard, however, to the maintenance of human rights of prisoners. The State recognises that a prisoner loses his rignt to liberty but maintain his residuary rights. It shall be the endeavour of the State to protect these residuary rights of the prisoners.

14. The State shall provide free legal aid to all needy prisoners.

15. Prisons are not the places for confinement of children. Children (boys under 16 years of age and girls under 18 years of age) shall in no case be sent to prisons. All children confined in prisons at present shall be transferred forthwith to appropriate institutions, meant exclusively for children with facilities for their care, education, training and rehabilitation. Benefit of non-institutional facilities shall, whenever possible be extended to such children.

16. Young offenders (between 16 to 23 years in the case of boys and 18 to 23 in the case of girls) shall not be confined in prisons meant for adult offenders. There shall be separate institutions for them where, in view of their young and impres-

sionable age, they shall be given treatment and training suited to their special needs of rehabilitation.

17. Women offenders shall, as far as possible, be confined in separate institutions specially meant for them. Wherever such arrangements are not possible they shall be kept in separate annexes of prisons with proper arrangements. The staff for these institutions and annexes shall comprise women employees only. Women prisoners shall be protected against all exploitation. Work and treatment programmes shall be devised for them in consonance with their special needs.

18. No non-criminal lunatic shall be confined in prisons. The law shall be suitably amended for the purpose. Proper arrangements shall be made for the care and treatment of criminal lunatics.

19. Persons courting arrest during non-violent socio-political economic agitations for declared public cause shall not be confined in prisons along with other prisoners. Separate prison camps with proper and adequate facilities shall be provided for such non-violent agitators.

20. Most of the persons sentenced to life imprisonment at present have to undergo at least 14 years of actual imprisonment. Prolonged incarceration has a degenerating effect on such persons and is not necessary either from the point of view of individual's reformation or from that of the protection of society. The term of sentence for life in such cases shall be made flexible in terms of actual confinement so that such a person may not necessarily to spend 14 years in prison and may be released when his incarceration is no longer necessary.

21. Prison service shall be developed as a professional career service. The State shall endeavour to develop a well-organised prison cadre based on appropriate job requirements, sound training and proper promotional avenues. The efficient functioning of prisons depends undoubtedly upon the personal qualities, educational qualifications, professional competence and character of prison personnel. The status, emoluments and other service conditions of prison personnel should be commensurate with their job requirements and responsibilities. An all India service namely the Indian Prisons and Correc-

tional Service shall be constituted to induct better qualified and talented persons at higher echelons. Proper training facilities for prison personnel shall be developed at the national, regional and state levels.

22. The State shall endeavour to secure and encourage voluntary participation of the community in prison programmes and in non-institutional treatment of offenders on an extensive and systematic basis. Such participation is necessary in view of the objective of ultimate rehabilitation of the offenders in the community. The government shall open avenues for such participation and shall extend financial and other assistance to voluntary organisations and individuals willing to extend help to prisoners and ex-prisoners.

23. Prisons are hitherto a closed world. It is necessary to open them to some kind of positive and constructive public discernment. Selected eminent public-men shall be authorised to visit prisons and give independent report on them to appropriate authorities.

24. In order to provide a forum in the community for continuous thinking on problems of prisons, for promoting professional knowledge and for generating public interest in the reformation of offenders, it is necessary that a professional non-official registered body is established at the national level. It may have its branches in the States and Union Territories. The Government of India, the State Governments and the Union Territory Administrations shall encourage setting up of such a body and its branches, and shall provide necessary financial and other assistance for their proper functioning.

25. Probation, aftercare, rehabilitation and follow-up of offenders shall form an integral part of the functions of the Department of Prisons and Correctional Services.

26. The development of prisons shall be planned in a systematic manner keeping in view the objectives and goals to be achieved. The progress of the implementation of such plans shall be continuously monitored and periodically evaluated.

27. The governments at the Centre and in the States/Union territories shall endeavour to provide adequate resources for the development of prisons and other allied services.

28. Government recognizes that the process of reformation and rehabilitation of offenders is an integral part of the total process of social reconstruction, and, therefore, the development of prisons shall find a place in the national development plans.

29. In view of the importance of uniform development of prisons in the country the Government of India has to play an effective role in this field. For this purpose the Central Government shall set up a high status National Commission on Prisons on a permanent basis. This shall be a specialised body to advise the Government of India, the State Governments and the Union Territory Administrations on all matters relating to prisons and allied services. Adequate funds shall be placed at the disposal of this Commission for enabling it to play an effective role in the development of prisons and other programmes. The Commission shall prepare an annual national report on the administration of prisons and allied services, which shall be placed before the Parliament for discussion.

30. As prisons form part of the criminal justice system and the functioning of other branches of the system—the police, the prosecution and the judiciary have a bearing on the working of prisons, it is necessary to effect proper coordination among these branches. The government shall ensure such coordination at various levels.

31. The State shall promote research in the correctional field to make prison programmes more effective.

A SELECT BIBLIOGRAPHY

Government Publications and Reports : Indian

Government of India : **Report of the Prison Discipline Committee, 1836-38.*

——**Howell's Note on Jails and Jail Discipline in India,* 1867-68.

——**Report of Indian Jail Conference,* 1877.

——*National Archives of India, *Documents connected with Prisons Act, 1894,* Legislative Deptt. Proceeding No. 164-271.

——**Report of the Indian Jails Committee,* 1919-20.

——*Reckless, Walter C., *Jail Administration in India,* (mimeographed), 1953.

——*Report of the All India Jail Manual Committee,* 1957-59.

——**Model Prison Manual,* 1960.

——**Report of the Working Group on Prisons,* 1972-73 (mimeographed).

——* *Report of Justice M.M. Ismail Commission,* 1977.

——**Report of the All India Committee on Jail Reforms* (Chairman : Justice A.N. Mulla), 1980-83, Vol. I and II.

——**Report of National Expert Committee on Women Prisoners* (Chairman : Justice Krishna Iyer), 1987, Vol. I and II.

Law Commission of India : **Seventy-seventh Report on Delay and Arrears in Trial Courts,* 1978.

——**Seventy-eighth Report on Congestion of Undertrial Prisoners in Jails,* 1979.

——*One Hundred and Fourteenth Report on Gram Nyayalaya 1986.

——*One Hundred and Sixteenth Report on National Judicial Services, 1986.

——*One Hundred and Seventeenth Report on Training of Judicial Officers, 1986.

——*One Hundred Twentieth Report on Manpower Planning in Judiciary, 1987.

——*One Hundred Twenty First Report on A New Forum for Judicial Appointments, 1987.

Government of India : National Police Commission, Tour Note No. 15, December 1978, "The Undertrials Of India," K.F. Rustamji.

Government of India : *Bureau of Police Research and Development, *Crime in India*, Annual Reports.

——*Central Bureau of Correctional Services, *Probation and Prisons : A Statistical Analysis*, 1972.

**Economic Survey*, 1974-75.

——*Report of the Seventh Finance Commission*, 1977-78, Chap. 10.

Government of West Bengal : *Home (Jails) Deptt., *Report of the West Bengal Jail Code Revision Committee*, (Chairman : Sukhomoy Dutt), 1972-73.

——*Report of the West Bengal Jail Reforms Committee* (Chairman : Tarapada Lahiri 1978-80.

——*Finance Deptt., *Civil Budget Estimates of the Govt. of West Bengal*, 1955-56 to 1979-80.

Government Publications and Reports : Foreign

Association of State Correctional Administrators, South Carolina Deptt. of Corrections, Columbia, USA ; *Uniform Correctional Policies and Procedures*, 1972.

Legislative Council of Maryland, Baltimore : *Report of the Committee on Capital Punishment*, 1962.

USA Bureau of Prisons : * *Correctional Institution : Design and Construction.*

——*The Jail : Its Operation aud Management.*

——*Classification of Jail Prisoners.*

HMSO, London : **Report of the Departmental Committee on Persistent Offenders*, 1932.

——*Report of the Royal Commission on Capital Punishment*, 1949-53, reprint 1973.

——*Report of Franklin Committee to Review Punishments in Prisons, Borstal Institutions, Approved Schools and Remand Homes*, 1951.

Report of Maxwell Committee on Discharged Prisoners' Aid Societies, 1953, reprint 1961.

——**Alternatives to Short Terms of Imprisonment* : Report of the Advisory Council on the Treatment of Offenders, 1957, reprint 1971.

——**Time Spent Awaiting Trial* : A Home Office Research Unit Report, 1960.

——**Report of the Inter-Departmental Committee on the Business of the Criminal Courts*, 1961.

——**Work for Prisoners* : Report of the Advisory Council on the Employment of Prisoners, 1961, reprint 1970.

——**Report of the Departmental Committee on the Probation Service*, 1962.

——**Work and Vocational Training in Borstals (England and Wales)* : Report of the Advisory Council on the Employment of Prisoners. 1962.

——**Preventive Detention* : Report of the Advisory Council on the Treatment of Offenders, 1963.

——**Some Statistical aud Other Numerical Techniques for Classifying Individuals* : A Home Office Research Unit Report, 1965.

——**The Organisation of After Care* : Report of the Advisory Council of the Treatment of Offenders, 1963, reprint 1966.

——**Studies of Female Offenders* : A Home Office Research Unit Report, 1967.

——**The Place of Voluntary Service in After-Care* : Second Report of the Working Party, 1967.

Ministry of Justice, Japan : **Correction and Rehabilitation of Offenders.*

——**Correctional Institutions in Japan.*

Books/Monographs

AHUJA, Ram. *Female Offenders in India*, Merrut, 1969.

AIR Commentaries. *The Constitution of India*, 2nd edn., 1970.

ALEXANDER, Myrl E. *Jail Administration*, Illinois : Thomas, 1957.

AMERICAN CORRECTIONAL ASSOCN. New York;**Handbook on Classification in Correctional Institutions, 1947*

——**Handbook on Pre-Release Preparation in Correctional Institutions*, 1950.

Manual for Correctional Standards, 1968.

BANERJEE, Pramathanath, *Public Administration in Ancient India*, London ; Macmillan, 1916.

BARNES, Harry E. & TEETERS, Negley K. *New Horizons In Criminology*, Indian edn. 1966.

BARNES, Harry E. *Society in Transition*, New York, 1939.

BARKER, F.A. *The Modern Prison System of India.* London : Macmillan, 1944.

BHATTACHARYA, B.K. *Prisons*, Calcutta : S.C. Sarkar, 1958.

BHUSAN, Vidya. *Prison Administration in India*, Delhi : S. Chand, 1970.

BOWKER, Lee H. *Prison Victimization*, New York, Oxford : Elsevier, 1980.

BUHLER, G. *The Laws of Manu*, Oxford, 1886.

BYE, R.T. *Capital Punishment in the United States*, Philadelphia, 1919.

CALVERT, E.R. *Capital Punishment in the Twentieth Century*, London, 1927.

CHADHA, Kumkum. *The Indian Jail : A Contemporary Document*, Delhi : Vikas, 1983.

CHANDRA, Devendra. *Open Air Prisons : A Sociological Study*, Allahabad : Vohra, 1984.

CLEMMER, Donald. *The Prison Community*, New York : Holt, Rinehart & Winston, 1958.

CRESSEY, Donald R. (ed.) *The Prison : Studies in Institutional Organization and Change*, 1961.

CHAMBER OF COMMERCE OF THE UNITED STATES. *Marshalling Citizen Power to Modernize Corrections.*

(monograph) reprint : American Correctional Association, 1972.

DATIR, R.N. *Prison as a Social System.* Bombay : Popular, 1978.

DRESSLER, David. *Practice and Theory of Probation and Parole,* 2nd edn., 2nd printing, 1971.

ELKIN, W.A. *The English Penal System,* 1957.

EVANS, Peter. *Prison Crisis,* London : George Allen & Unwin, 1980.

ENCYCLOPEDIA AMERICANA, Vol. 21, 1973.

ENCYCLOPAEDIA BRITANNICA, Vol. 18, 1967.

FOX, Lionel W. *The English Prison and Borstal System,* London, 1952.

GIBBONS, Don C. *Society, Crime, and Criminal Carriers,* Delhi : Prentice Hall, 3rd edn., 1978.

GILLIN, John L. *Criminology and Penology,* New York, 3rd edn. 1945. *Taming the Criminal,* New York, 1931.

GLASER, David, *The Effectiveness of a Prison and Parole System,* 1964.

GOLDFARB, Ronald R. & SINGER, Linda R. *After Conviction,* New York, 1973.

GRAY, Francis C. *Prison Discipline in America,* London, 1948.

GRUNHUT, Max, *Penal Reform : A Comparative Study,* Oxford : Clarendon Press, 1948.

IVES, George. *A History of Penal Methods,* London, 1934.

JOHNSON, Elmer H. *Crime, Correction and Society,* Illinois, 1968.

JOLLY, Julius. Tr., Ghosh, Balakrishna, *Hindu Law and Custom,* 1928.

JONES, Howard. *Crime and Penal System,* 1956.

KAUFMANN, Walter. *Without Guilt and Justice.*

KAUTILYA. *Arthasastra,* Tr. Shamasastry, R., 6th edn. 1960.

KING, Roy D. & MORGAN, Rod. *The Future of the Prison System,* Westmead (England) ; Gower, 1980.

KIRCHHEIMER, Otto & RUSCHE, Georg. *Punishment and Social Structure,* New York, 1939.

KLARE, H.J. *Anatomy of Prisons,* London : Hutchinson, 1960.

KNUDTEN, Richard D. *Crime in a Complex Society*, Illinois, 1970.

KOESTLER, Arthur. *Reflections on Hanging*. New York, 1957.

LOCKWOOD, Daniel. *Prison Sexual Violence*, New York : Elsevier, 1980.

LOPEZ-REY, Manuel. *Crime : An Analytical Appraisal*, London, 1970.

MAZUMDAR, Sudha. *Women in Prison at Home And Abroad* (Monograph), Calcutta : Orient Longman, 1957.

MIDDENDORFF, Wolf. *New Forms of Juvenile Delinquency : Their Origin, Prevention and Treatment*, 1960.

MITRA, N.L. *Juvenile Delinquency and Indian Justice System*, Delhi : Deep & Deep, 1988.

MORRIS, Norval. *The Future of Imprisonment*, London, 1974.

NAYAR, Kuldip. *In Jail*, Delhi : Vikas, 1978.

RAO, S. Venugopal. *Facets of Crime in India*, Bombay : Allied, 1967. *Dynamics of Crime*, Delhi : IIPA.

RECKLESS, Walter C. *The Crime Problems*, 1st Indian edn. 1971.

ROSE, Gordon. *The Struggle for Penal Reform*, London, 1961.

SELIGMAN, Edwin R.R. (ed.) *Encyclopaedia of Social Sciences*, 15th Printing, 1963, Vol. VII.

SELLIN, Thorsten. *The Death Penalty*, Philadelphia, 1959.

SEN, Prosanto K. *From Punishment to Prevention*, Oxford Univ. Press, 1932.

SHUKLA, K.S. *Adolescent Thieves : A Study in Socio-Cultural Dynamics*, Delhi : Leela, 1979.

SINGH, Indra J. *Indian Prison : A Sociological Enquiry*, Delhi : Concept 1979.

SRIVASTAVA, S.P. *The Indian Prison Community*, Lucknow : Pustak Kendra, 1977.

SUTHERLAND, Edwin H. & CRESSEY, Donald R. *Principles of Criminology*, 2nd. Indian reprint, 1968.

TAFT, Donald R. & ENGLAND, Ralph W., Jr. *Criminology*, New York, 1964.

TAPPAN, Paul W. (ed.). *Contemporary Correction*, New York, London : McGraw-Hill, 1951.

TRIVEDI, B.V. *Prison Administration In India : Model Prison Programmes in UP*, Delhi : Uppal, 1987.

WILSON, Joseph G. *Are Prisons Necessary ?*, Philadelphia, 1950.

WILSON, Margaret, *The Crime of Punishment*, New York, 1931.

WINES, Frederick, H. *Punishment and Reformation*, New York, 1923.

WOLFF, Michael. *Prisons*, U.K., 1967.

Articles

AHUJA, Ram. "A Prisoner is a Human Being", *Times Weekly*, Bombay, May 27, 1973.

BALL, John C. "The Deterrence Concept in Criminology and Law" *The Journal of Criminal Lew, Criminology And Police Science*, Northwestern Univ. School of Law, Vol. 44, No. 3, 1955.

BRAND, Chris. "How Radical Are Our Alternatives to Prison ?", *New Society*, U.K., January, 18, 1973.

BAILEY, Donald R. "Advisory Arbitration : Approach to Solving Inmate Grievances", *Indian Journal of Criminology*, Vol. 15, No. 1, 1987.

CELLEINI, H.R. Hank. "The Management and Treatment of Institutionalised Violent Aggressors", *Indian Journal of Criminology*, Vol. 14; No. 2. 1986.

CARLSON, Rich J. "Rehabilitating Criminals", *Center Magazine* USA, July-Aug. 1973.

DIAZ, S.M. "Prison Administration in India", *Indian Journal of Public Administration*, Vol. XXV, No. 1, Jan-March, 1979.

GANDHI, Arun. "Crime in India", *Illustrated Weekly*, June 3, 1973.

GUHA-ROY, Jaytilak. "Role of Voluntary Agencies in Prevention of Crime and Treatment of Offenders", *Indian Journal of Public Administration*, Vol. XXXIII, No. 3, July-Sept., 1987.

——"The Role of Public in the After-Care of Discharged Offenders", *The Journal of Correctional Work*, No. XXIII, 1977.

——"Cleansing of the Jails", *The Statesman*, Calcutta, March 14, 1983.

——"Humanizing the Mode of Execution", *The Statesman* Calcutta/Delhi, May 27, 1982.

——"Education Benind Bars", *The Statesman*, Calcutta, August 3, 1981.

——"Helping Young Delinquents", *The Statesman*, Calcutta, March 30, 1981.

HANDA, R.L. "Reflections on Objectives of Imprisonment", Editorial article, *Indian Journal of Criminology*, Vol. 14, No. 1, 1986.

HIRANANDANI, L.H. "The Sentence of Death", *Illustrated Weekly*, August 29, 1976.

JACOBS, James B. "The Politics of Correction : Town/Prison Relations as a Determinant of Reform", *Social Service Review*, USA, December, 1976.

JOHNSON, Elmer H. "Selective Factors in Capital Punishment", *Social Forces*, December 1957.

JUCHAU, R.H. "A Policy for Adult Education in Penal Institutions", *Australian Journal of Social Issues*, February, 1973.

KALHAN, Promilla. "Towards Gender Justice", *The Hindustan Times*, June 15, 1987.

KARLE, Kenneth E. "Educating Prisoners", *New Society*, July 5, 1973.

KARPMAN, Benjamin, "Criminality, Insanity and the Law", *Journal of Criminal Law and Criminology*, January-February 1949.

KARKARIA, Bachi J. "The Agony of Idleness", *The Statesman*, Feburary 2 and 3, 1981.

MAZUMDAR, Sudha, "Rehabilitation of Female Offenders" (mimeographed) presented at a Training Workshop for Correctional Services, held at Calcutta on March 29, 1974 (unpublished).

MCCORMICK, Austin, "The Prisons' Role in Crime Prevention", *Journal of Criminal Law and Criminology*, Vol. XLV. 1950-51.

MOHANTY, Amarendra & HAZARY, Narayan. "Evolution of Prison Administration and Reform in India : The Orissa

Scene", *Indian Journal of Public Administration*, Vol. XXXI No. 4. October-Dec., 1985.

MOHANTY, S. "Convicts and Their Level of Religiosity : A Study in the Three District Headquarters Jails of Western Orissa", *Indian Journal of Criminology*, Vol. 14, No. 1, 1986.

MORIYAMA, T. & SALAMA, A. "Citizens Association and the Volunteer Probation Officer", *Informal Mechanism of Crime : A Cross-Cultural Perspective*, United Nations Social Defence Research Institute, 1988.

PANAKAL, J.J. "Indian Prison and Correctional Services", Editorial article, *Indian Journal of Criminology*, Vol. 14, No. 2, 1986.

PRAKASH, S. "Jail Administration in the Country", *The Journal of Correctional Work*, No. XXIII, 1977.

RAHULA, Andhra, "Prisoners of Conscience", *Illustrated Weekly*, March 23, 1675.

RAMACHANDRA S. & RAMAN, Suma. "Creativity in Habitual Prisoners", *Indian Journal of Criminology*, Vol. 14, No. 1, 1986.

RAO, Venugopal S. "Issues on Abolition of Capital Punishment", CBI Bulletin, March 1973.

RAY, D.N. "The Probation Approach", *The Journal of Correctional Work*, No. XVII, 1971.

RAJ, A.S. New Horizons of Prison Reforms In India", *The Journal of Correctional Work*, No. XXIII, 1977.

SAHAY, S. "Behind the Prison Walls", *The Statesman*, April 12, 1979.

SANYAL, S. & THOMAS, G. "A Comparative Study of Prisoners of Open Camps and Closed Prisons in U.P. Regarding Self-Esteem and Attitude Towards Co-inmates", *Indian Journal of Criminology*, Vol. 16, No. 1, 1988.

SHRIVASTAVA, R.S. "Formation and Functioning of Friendship Groups : A Sociological Study among Prison Inmates", *Sociological Bulletin*, March 1973.

SHIVARAMAKRISHNA, K. "Improvement in Prison Administration", *Lok Rajya*, January 1, 1973.

SHUKLA, K.S. "Role of Police In Juvenile Justice", *Indian*

Journal of Criminology, and Criminalistics, Vol. 1, No. 3 & 4. 1981.

SIKKA, K.D. "Prison: How Far A Treatment Institution", *The Journal of Correctional Work*, No. XXIII, 1977.

SINGH, Hira, Correctional Training And Research", Editorial article, *The Journal of Correctional Work*, No. XVIII, 1971.

SINGH, D.R. and JATAR, D.P. "Attitude of Prison Inmates Towards Facilities and Amenities Offered to Them", *The Journal of Correctional Work*. No. XXIII, 1977.

SRINIVASAN, S. "Correction and Rehabilitation: Extent and Scope of Community Involvement", *The Journal of Correctional Work*, No. XVIII, 1977.

SRIVASTAVA, R.S. "Prison : Some Organisational Aspects", *The Journal of Correctional Work*, No. XXIII, 1977.

SRIVASTAVA, S.P. "The Quality of Basic Necessities in Prison", *Indian Journal of Social Work*, January, 1973.

——"Sex life in an Indian Male Prison", *Indian Journal of Social Work*, April 1974.

——"Planning a Strategy for the Prevention and Control of Juvenile Delinquency in India", *The Journal of Correctional Work*, No. XXIII, 1977.

SOHNI, Neera Kuckreja. "Women in Prison", *Illustrated Weekly*, August 25, 1974.

SUBRAMANIAM, M.A. "How Probation can Reduce Recidivism", *The Journal of Correctional Work*, No. XVII. 1971.

SURI, S.K. "Rehabilitation of Offenders : Role of Police", *The Journal of Correctional Work*, No. XVII, 1971.

TANDON, S.L. "Probation ; View-Point of the Community", *Indian Journal of Criminology*, Vol. 16, No. 1, 1988.

THILAGRAJ, R. "Goal Perception of Delinquents and non-delinquents", *Indian Journal of Criminology*, Vol. 15, No. 2, 1987.

TRIVEDI, B V. "Work Incentives in Indian Correctional Institutions", *The Journal of Correctional Work*, No. XXIII 1977.

INDEX